The Psychic Life of

GEORGE HERBERT LEIGH MALLORY

The Psychic Life of
GEORGE HERBERT LEIGH MALLORY

BOOK ONE

COPYRIGHT 2014

WITH EDITORIAL ASSISTANCE BY

LYN RAFE-LAWYER

AUTHOR OF "KEEP YOUR PECKER UP," "BRIEF

ENCOUNTERS," AND "LYN'S ASS LEGACY."

AN AUTOBIOGRAPHY BY

RAY EUGENE HARKLEROAD, JUNIOR

POST OFFICE BOX 5301 PALM SPRINGS, CALIFORNIA 92263

WORDWAG.COM 760-333-2196

GHLMALLORY@GMAIL.COM

authorHOUSE®

AuthorHouse™ LLC
1663 Liberty Drive
Bloomington, IN 47403
www.authorhouse.com
Phone: 1-800-839-8640

Published by AuthorHouse   02/24/2014

ISBN: 978-1-4918-5589-8 (sc)
ISBN: 978-1-4918-5588-1 (hc)
ISBN: 978-1-4918-5590-4 (e)

Library of Congress Control Number: 2014902215

Contents

Introduction

Perhaps it's odd to have a story as a sequel to a death and to still call it an autobiography, but this story is exactly that. I died, I was reborn, and now it is time to tell about it. Perhaps I should start with an introduction.

I am George Herbert Leigh Mallory still though known by a different name this lifetime—same soul, different body. You may not yet know my present name but that will soon become associated with the name I wore from 18 June 1886 to 8 June 1924. My prior life ended on a clear blue moment on that date in 1924 following an unexpected plunge from the near top of Mount Everest. My now unused body was found on the side of the mountain in 1999. I have a new body, born in East Tennessee in 1948. This is a remarkable story.

First let me ask you to set aside your expectations. If you are profoundly religious, there may be some difficulty dealing with the story I'm going to relate to you not because of what I have to say, but because you will be working from your belief system that likely interferes with the absorption of the details I need to convey. On the other hand, if you have ever questioned the precepts of your religion, feel free to understand my message.

One thing is true—I have stood before God and I have a very clear understanding of my relationship with Him. Let me say Him if you will—my description of God doesn't lend itself to a Him or Her, rather an It, but that is uncomfortable to say only because of the English language, not because there is any chance at all that God will be offended or that I will be incorrect in saying that.

George Herbert Leigh Mallory was a well educated man who lived and was schooled in England, later a Cambridge professor, and a man who thoroughly enjoyed France, loved his wife and family, and did so with all of his heart and soul. He was an adventurer, a man who even at the moment of this death turned to the inevitable and said "I'm not going to miss this." He never feared death and this event was not suicide but an accident, an error in the execution of a plan, perhaps a bit of vanity spiced with a moment of perplexing anticipation. George Herbert Leigh Mallory should have been the first man to climb Mount Everest if only because there had to be a first. George Mallory was not a competitive person other than to have a healthy ambition to succeed and to help those about him to succeed as well. Falling to my death from the North Face of Mount Everest was inconvenient. I really wanted to do so much more in that lifetime much as I have wanted to do so much more in this lifetime. Now must be that time. Any further delay is an affront to society I must remember—the effort is necessary and the impact is likely to be great. See, the concept of reincarnation offends some who stand so quickly on their soap box and proclaim the truth—or what they perceive as the truth. I am doing the same mind you, but I'll let you decide if the pieces fit into this jigsaw puzzle of eternity. Reincarnation is just part of the puzzle, but a vital necessary part of the puzzle if you wish to understand the makeup of the universe. The precepts of religion only get into the way—a true red herring to understanding and knowing truth if you must have it said bluntly.

Chapter One

I have known the circumstances of my prior life's death since I came into consciousness as a child. Before the age of three even, my dreams were always that fall. The sudden looseness—a lack of hard contact with anything. Then the rushing wind and the horizon and the landscape far below me. Then, ever so oddly, my body continues to fall below me as I watch from an airy vantage point and my realization of all things future and all things past. My view suddenly distracted by the two bright white points of light that appear next to me. That haunting view accompanied the falling of the arches in my feet—I've often wondered if I there was a connection, if perhaps I did land a bit on my feet and the body too carries over some knowledge of that ending just as the soul does. My mother dutifully rubbed my feet as a youngster, my arches in driving pain each evening, it seemed as the process wore on. The pain eventually subsided but the flat feet remain to this day.

At the age of four I recall saying clearly to myself that I had to keep this body more limber—it was not as flexible as the body I had previously. I was injured at about age two—I fell forward and struck my head at the hairline on a pyramid shaped rock changing not only my forehead where a small scar still exists, but also changing the timetable I was to deal with for the disclosure of my purpose on earth this go round.

There have been those persons when I relate the knowledge of who I was before my current lifetime that will ask "is everyone who remembers their prior lives famous?" Of course the question is daunting for many—why would almost everyone who claims to remember who they were previously always relate the name of someone famous. The answer is simply not as difficult to understand as might be expected, but unless some thought is given to the question the answer is not so easy to come. The answer becomes easy when it is understood that persons who are able to remember the successes of a prior life were successes because they sought and had the help of God in their endeavors. Only with God's help do you become famous (or profoundly excel), and only with God's blessing do you remember your prior life or lives unaided. It is that embracing of God that permits the success, the acknowledgement of the success, and likely the continuation of that success. The takeaway on this is simply that you must ask God, rely on God, and expect God to bring the bounty. It just works that way—it is not a concept—it is a law. The more you adhere to that law, the more you succeed in life. And for you that still believe that material things are the great determinant of a live well lived—see if you can equate that to spiritual advancement. For you that boast of how much money you have just know that God is watching carefully for what you do with it. Are you using it for good or for indulgences that you would rather no one else know?

You can leave God out of that last remark. God knows everything. So you thought Santa Claus was all knowing? Santa Claus knows when you've been naughty or nice—God on the other hand, knows why you were naughty or nice and gives you credit when your purposes, your intentions, were good, even if your plan for execution was less than stellar.

I'm still formulating the story I want to tell—it is a bit more difficult to explain the experiences of a life yet knowing that I'm going to have to refer not only to the history of this lifetime, but to the history of the last lifetime, and perhaps even earlier, but also to the history yet born of the future. I'll do my best—that is all any of us can do—I'll ask God to help and if I'm willing to accept it and keep my purposes clear and pure, then I'll achieve the clarity to explain the concept, the detail, and the purpose of all of this. God is good—but like the best set of tools in your garage—if you don't use them, then you've gained no value.

So, let us begin. The easiest way to begin is to be the child that we all began as for this sojourn on earth this time around. This special note is really to the parent, for they together either open the journey in hope, or resolutely slam the door on the prospect. Children carry not only the knowledge of their past lives but they carry the message of God, and often the ability to speak to the servants of God that sit at their shoulder each day or speak gently into their ear so often. Guardian Angels or as many spiritually inclined persons call them Guides, are spirits there to assist us in our earthly journey. These are the ones you really want to listen to—the ones that are ours, the ones that are there to help us. Too often we fail to listen to the ones we should and instead listen to the spirits who want to compel us to acts or actions contrary to our best interest, to acts contrary to law or morality. I'll address some steps you can take to discern the difference and to protect yourself in following chapters. One simple question provides the disclosure you really are looking for. Ask those who advise you if your instructions come from "God's will." Make sure that the source of the request is from the Most High—anything less is not acceptable.

Talents and proclivities brought from prior lives are more compelling than most parents would acknowledge or accept—but often fighting the very talents of the child damages for the lifetime as well as serving to sever the ties to the infinite. In other more simple terms, embrace the child for all that he or she is, and encourage the best aspects of the child. Inquire as to what was learned in that last lifetime, and ask simply and plainly what is to be learned in this lifetime. You might ask too if the child speaks to God—but don't be disappointed if the child will not tell you what is said to God.

Conversations with God are private, and often you'll cause the child to close up rather than to speak more by prodding or twisting for your own satisfaction. If possible during these conversations, record the questions and answers exchanged between you and the child. What you get piecemeal can be tied together for a more understandable and cohesive description later. And if nothing else, the child when older will be able to review those discussions to refresh the memory. It is that direct input of prior experience that is likely to result in the best remembrance of detail. Do your part to help the child out—you were selected by that soul to be the parent (in all likelihood) so go ahead—be a trooper—and do your part. You'll be surprised—not only are the children the future, but they are also the past. A rich, varied, wonderfully equipped past and fully available to function in this new world. Help them to reach their potential. While you are at it, do your part to re-establish your connection to your own past lives. Join a Spiritual Study Group if there is one in your area, or you might consider the Association for Research and Enlightenment (EdgarCayce.Org) in Virginia Beach, Virginia, or another such group that helps you learn and understand the tools of enlightenment. Those tools are meditation, meditation, and more meditation. Meditate often, sincerely, and with the best tools you can acquire. Those tools are books on self-hypnosis—get into the practice.

The book "The Sleeping Prophet" by Jess Stearn is probably the one of the best books available to have you understand the concepts of your physical incarnation. It is the biography of Edgar Cayce (who founded the Association for Research and Enlightenment in Virginia Beach, Virginia (b. 1877, d. 1945)) and is easy reading. The real benefit is that concepts of your existence are easily and relevantly presented, and the life of this man clearly made understandable and usable in your daily life. You'll understand re-incarnation, the source of the Universal Knowledge, and other spiritual concepts in a friendly, usable way.

Your association with God is not theoretical—know that and practice that. The thought that your association with God is theoretical is what has allowed religion to spread and undermine our true reality. God is available for you whenever and wherever you seek Him. Take the time to learn how to remove the barriers and know—know—know that there is nothing between you and God. Never has been—never will be, and that knowledge of your association with God bears repeating, repeating, repeating.

Chapter Two

When I was a child, I clearly recall my mother teaching me to read on her lap—a book spread open to pages that she helped me go through and understand the writing. No, it wasn't the popular aspect we get today: it was a real adult book with a religious bent and I recall pictures of angels flying in formation.

I knew clearly which angel was me—I pointed it out with pride to my mother who confirmed my assertion rather than trying to discourage it. I loved those sessions—and to say the least I learned to read at a very early age and with reading came writing. There was but one word that I ever recall being stumped on in school—I had just never come across it. The word was "debut"—and I did pronounce it incorrectly and of course failed on the meaning when reading out loud in class one day. I did the "de but" approach—I was quickly stopped and corrected by my teacher. That was the last time I recall having that sort of error. Even today, I receive a "Word of the Day" from one of the dictionary sites on the web. New words are always being added to our language—words coined to meet new circumstances and occasionally new meanings to old established words—or obscure words brought into the forefront to apply to previously unconsidered circumstances or applications.

In my last lifetime I spoke French, in this lifetime I studied Latin. With at least the three most recent lifetimes all being using English as the primary language, I've become comfortable and proficient and depending on the circumstance, direct and clear. It is a fact that the more people you need to reach immediately will demand an ability resulting in a higher standard of clarity. Understanding is a one-on-one mission.

Teach your children early of the language, concepts of their existence, and law of the land to make them more adept in their surroundings and more proficient in their dealings with others.

Being the adventurer and lecturer George Herbert Leigh Mallory and having died in a fall from the side of Mount Everest, there have been several books written on my prior life. I don't pretend to remember everything about that life or the lives preceding it, but there is enough information captured by those authors to remind me of similarities in lifetimes that have occurred then and now. Take for example my rejection as George of the very teachings of my father, a minister of religion.

I rejected the church then and I reject the church now. There was no substance, no logic to what I saw as religion. It was not the pomp and circumstance that failed to impress me; it was the skewing of concept from adoration of our creator to adoration of "trusted servants" who in the application of faith could not be trusted. No, I'm not referring to the scandals of the clergy that sullied the Catholic Church in the 20th and beginning of the 21th Century, but rather that an attitude of "I know—you don't" and "I cannot lead you to knowing" that I rejected. In this lifetime, I walked away from the Presbyterian Church one day when I was ten years of age.

My brother Jack and I had gone to church in an old stone church on Bristol Road in what today is known as Bensalem, Pennsylvania. This is a colonial area and many places claim that George Washington slept there, especially the Red Lion Inn in Andalusia if the place still exists, and I trust it does as it is a historical landmark.

My brother is 18 months younger than I, and we both were frequently sent to the Bible class at the church—my mother sometimes attending and my father seldom attending. The church was close enough that walking to the church was a short 15 minutes or so away, and we were with other children of our age group. Being originally from East Tennessee, Kingsport, from where my family moved in about 1950, a strong orientation to Bible study existed. That part of Tennessee is often known as the "Buckle of the Bible Belt" with the snake handlers, the holy rollers, and other sects in relatively close proximity to the area. My father was from Kingsport, my mother from more of a region known as Hawkins County.

I know they were married at age 17, and my father served in World War Two in Europe. He seldom spoke of that—whatever transpired in the theatre of war was not a memory he chose to recollect without incredible prodding. I never really heard it. My father did participate in a program to record his recollections before so many of those heroes died as the years bore on them—a patriotism program. I've never been able to bring myself to listen to the narration though I have a copy. I am personally anti-war. After all, war only serves to kill. I've yet to understand the nobility in killing and profoundly question the wisdom of the United States entering Afghanistan to attack a country when the perpetrators of an act of war lived in rocks, well outside of the government control. And as we have learned, it was likely the adjoining country of Pakistan that actually gave Osama Bin Laden comfort—not the Afghanis. Just what did all of those innocent civilians do to deserve death? Make that a double when it comes to the war in Iraq—if not for the slight George Walker Bush felt had been placed on his father, George H.W. Bush, the 41st President of the United States by Saddam Hussein, I am sure we would not have attacked that country. The wisdom of not attacking became startling clear when Idiot George made his proclamation that indeed, there were no weapons of mass destruction in the country. But oh well, let's beat the hell out of them anyway. I am paraphrasing, but the outcome of his orders as the Commander in Chief of the Armed Forces of the United States of America is not in doubt. We attacked viciously, killing civilians, destroying historical landmarks, and eventually removing the barriers between sects of Islamists in the country held in check for so long by the existing government and allowing harsh civil strife to result.

I have a few tidbits to share about George Walker Bush later in the book—but you, dear reader, will find a very harsh opinion about him from me and, Dear George, please note that your attempts to intimidate me were hugely unsuccessful. My standard thought on the subject is always "What are you going to do about it? Kill Me? Is that your best shot?" Read on, dear reader—the best is yet to come.

Continuing with the narration—I enjoyed the company of the others in the Bible Class and we would read from the Bible from time to time as would be logical. I stopped going one day when I was incredibly shaken by what happened on that Sunday—it seemed so simple but I just didn't want to deal with it. I could not share it with anyone, and I didn't know what to do. As I opened the Bible I was suddenly confronted with a moving picture—a full page moving picture of someone walking on a sandy background—sandals and feet moving step by step in the Bible. It was almost as if I were looking down at my own two feet. I could sense others around me but didn't see them in the picture. I was shaken—it was my first experience, I think, dealing with a vision in this life but so much has happened since.

I was running from the truth, I fear, as I never went back to that church even though, if recalled correctly, I was to be a Bible teacher at the tender age of 10 years. One thing was sure—I am pretty certain that the others in the class didn't have the same visual experience I had.

The bulk of my school experiences up to at least the age of 17 seemed pretty normal—I had inclinations, visions, knowledge of the forthcoming but didn't share them often or strongly. They didn't seem that relevant at the time, and more importantly, only served to bring me ridicule—a harsh slap at that point in adolescent growth. There are some stories worth repeating.

My brother brought a new understanding to me when I was eleven and had sent away for one of those items on the back cover of a comic book. "Hypnotize your friends" the advertisement said, and I was intrigued.

My best friend and the best friend of my brother too I would venture, was Peter MacDonough who lived just up the street from us there in Bensalem, in the area near King David Cemetery and the field where now the Neshaminy Mall stands. My brother who was a scant nine years of age, was the victim for my experiment in hypnosis—and all I did was to follow the simple directions, speak easily and comfortably, and have a thought about what I wanted to accomplish with the session.

Being just a bit mean, the intent was to regress my brother to a previous time in his life, where a budding nine year old would bawl like a baby.

Seemed simple enough so we set out on the venture to take my brother back just a little in time enough to have him bawl. Isn't that what mean older brothers do anyway? My brother Jack (he went by his middle name at the time) agreed and I set out to hypnotize him with Peter at my side. We both found it greatly humorous—but that was the whole point anyway.

As I twirled the little disc in front of my brothers eyes, carefully following the directions that came with the disc, it went on in a very monotonous drone—"You are getting sleepy", and I repeated "You are getting sleepy" and over and over and over again. After a few minutes my brother seemed to fall lightly asleep and his head dropped but that was success—not failure—we were hypnotizing my brother and my instructions came in dull tones so to not disrupt the hypnotic state. You are going back, I said, you are going back. And back he went. We never considered anything other than the current lifetime.

When we went back, suddenly he started crying with an incredible intensity and we just had to ask "why are you crying?" The reply was shocking: "I killed two people." Well, my brother was nine years of age—he certainly did not kill anyone. What was he talking about? Who are you, I asked without thought—and the reply came "I am Ivan, the Tsar of Russia!" We were shocked—somehow we had gone from this lifetime to the previous, and as children, really did not know where we had gone, or why we had gone there. This was only a joke but it seemed to have gone well astray. We took that bit of information—the name Ivan, Russia, and Tsar—and quickly counted up as the comic book hypnosis toy instructions told us to, telling my brother that he was returning to a conscious state—we were certainly relieved when he opened his eyes and failed to understand that anything was wrong. Then the quest began.

Running up the basement stairs, I and friend Peter with Jack trailing shortly behind wondering what was going on, quickly found the necessary volume of the encyclopedia in the hallway bookcase that listed Ivan—the Tsar of Russia.

"Ivan the Terrible" declared the page, and we went on to read about that person in history that we had never before encountered. Even at that time and to this day, my brother disclaims what we found, but I see it as simply not remembering what he had said and the information found when he was under that hypnotic state. I ponder today that my period between lifetimes is twenty four years for my most recent incarnation. My brother's reflects a period much, much longer. The full name is Ivan IV Vasilyevich, born 25 August 1530 and meeting his death on 28 March 1584. Ivan ruled Russia from 1533 until his death in 1584. That would make his period between incarnations to be 365 years. The time between incarnations is more purposeful than on earth I assume—and surely more valued for quality and control of spiritual advancement. I only wish I could reflect more on it. My meeting with God will suggest some things—but even there the full purpose is beyond my meager ability to understand all that I experienced.

Not too far beyond the experience with hypnosis with my brother was also a spontaneous reading for a friend from High School, a charming young lady by the name of Carmen Pannacio. Her reading spanned her entire life from the age of 17 forward, and from what I have been able to confirm now that Carmen is well along in her career and life I was right on the mark as disclosed in the reading.

Carmen got her reading at a party at my home—we had a large basement and on occasion would host parties for my high schools friends. We didn't have the problems of drugs and alcohol—my high school friends respected the law, and would not have assumed that violating those laws were in any way OK. In fact, I recall that I was not even aware of marijuana until I was 19—that would be post high school, and my employment put me firmly on the other side of the issue as a police dispatcher.

Carmen is a delightful person—doing well today from what I hear, but I don't recall speaking to her anytime after high school graduation. I made several efforts to reach her a few years back and in doing so, got confirmation of the detail I had provided at that young age. It was sometime about 2005 I was working in my home office in Miramar, Florida, when very clear recollection occurred prompting me to verify what I had said to Carmen.

I was sitting on a sofa when the memory of that reading resurfaced and it was as if I was giving it for the first time back in 1965. It is strange—almost as if a string or coil suddenly unwound and I could see and feel all of the detail before me again—just as I had done so then.

At the party, I had told Carmen that we were soul mates, knowing that soul mates are those persons who have had prior interaction. Don't try to apply so many criteria to the definition of soul mates, it really is the knowledge that one soul needs to interact with another on the earth plane. It can be long or short, happy or awkward, with clear purpose and understanding, or knowledge that the two of you are associated but you just have to wonder why. In other words, sometimes just running into each other meets the criteria.

Carmen was everyone's sweetheart—a fine person and a lovely person. Her reading was spontaneous—a surprise to me at that stage in my life but a process that has become more comfortable for me as it has occurred several times in my life now, usually with profound results. Sometimes the spontaneous readings has been for individuals that I didn't know beforehand, and don't know what transpired after the reading, and sometimes the spontaneous reading has resulted in my seeing the results or confirmation of that reading in persons who have become famous.

That scenario fits my meeting and spontaneous reading of David Bromstad, who now stars on his own show, Color Splash: Miami, on the cable television network HGTV (Home and Garden Television).

Carmen sat on a stool next to me in my basement of the family home the evening of her unexpected reading. My brother and I were having a party and the music was playing. Readings are occasionally controllable, but generally are almost a "push" from the other side as I feel the information coming and do my best to put it out there before it is lost. I've equated the feeling to being a hose, and the hose doesn't know when the water is coming, it is just prepared to direct the water to whatever destination is needed. I neither create nor am I able to hold onto much of what is said often other than the gist of the reading. Specific phrases are sometimes held and that aspect has proven most valuable in recounting and confirming the positive nature of the reading. For Carmen, a whole life reading resulted. As a high school student, Carmen got the blueprint of her upcoming life. Whether I read what she was going to do, or she chose to do what was read is always a question, but I have learned that the pattern had been set and has played out.

Carmen was advised that she would become a teacher, in fact an art teacher as I told her "I hope that you like art because you will become an art teacher", a very good one, and a teacher to whom awards would be given. Further, she would be the mother of two boys, and her married name would be Slivinski. I cautioned Carmen that the name Slivinski might be in error in that it might be Slavinski as I had never heard of the former name, but did hear of the latter. Turns out that I was right in what I related, the married name is Slivinski.

Two boys were her off-spring, and I also said that her husband would die about a year and a half before I attempted to contact her. I knew then that it was better to say that the husband would die rather than to say that there might be a separation, which I understand has been the actual case. The reason was that Carmen was not to be dissuaded from the marriage if knowing that it would end in separation. Too, I told her that we would be in contact in Florida many years in the future.

Carmen did live and work in Florida, not too far from me in South Florida, but I only became aware of her employment there after she had moved to Central Florida. My attempts to reach her directly have been unsuccessful, Carmen choosing apparently not to re-establish the friendship. The life reading was correct though and I know that she has had a happy, successful, and fulfilling life.

Many of my classmates in junior and senior high schools were somewhat problematic—capped by my senior year employment as a police dispatcher for the local police department. That job was the equivalent of the current 911 Police Dispatcher, mandating me to take a very serious view towards the work I did, and teaching me the importance of detail in work.

I learned too not to be too emotional but rather to look very objectively at my efforts and circumstances around me. Besides the police cars, which I eventually came to mentally place them in the various areas of patrol in the 22 square mile township adjoining Philadelphia, I handled the dispatch of the seven local volunteer fire departments. I enjoyed that work, and after leaving at age 22 I felt a great deal of a letdown in whatever else I was employed in.

Police work is important, and despite some media accounts, I will say that the professionals are well trained, dedicated, and honest. There will always be exceptions I'm sure, but for any group of people to tackle the truly oddball people that police have to deal with on any given day is truly a test of that commitment. Even in my small bailiwick there were outstanding examples of true heroism—and examples of sadness too. Friends I had know in school getting arrested for marijuana possession, or another friend for being AWOL, or another for accidentally hitting and causing the death of a pedestrian while driving. The police officers, detectives, and the chief were all very dedicated—it did seem as their lives revolved around their work—a public service work seldom matched by any other profession.

Being as serious and more focused as I had become did make me the brunt of a few jokes but I took serious pride in my work. If nothing else, I never entered a bar until I was 21—the legal age then in Pennsylvania, nor did I try marijuana until I had left the department. Being twenty one, there was a certain expectation that I would apply for the force, but being only 135 pounds at 5'6" was the strongest reason not to consider the force. Some of the people brought in on charges were simply huge and I saw no practical way that I could ever handle others of that size. No, a job requiring physical force or might was not a likely profession for me. I left the force at age 22—the timing came during a salary change, but it had to come anyway.

My psychic insight was always acute though I didn't really understand or realize the nature of that gift until later, even though I shared visions, prophesies, or whatever else came through with others just as it happened. Part of the reason I never became as honed in the subject as I should was probably a lack of language for the phenomena. Today, with my knowledge of Edgar Cayce, with television shows devoted to aspects of psychic phenomena, and a, pardon the expression, devil may care attitude of youth; the impact of what I shared was not as well understood as it might have been.

I saw, and I shared, and what you did with the information given you was your concern. Certainly, it was not my concern. And I did little to follow up on it back then. Too, I used to get more detail that related to individuals rather than what has come to be today. My information today relates to global events, or what will be national news in a short period.

Some of the strange events from my youth included a fall into a swimming pool, and knowledge of my future spouse for starters.

The fall into a swimming pool when I was only about eight years of age and before I had learned to swim brought a voice from the other side that said very, very clearly: "Let Him Drown." I thought to myself, "Boy, this is going to be a strange and difficult lifetime," but the thought was quickly removed as my uncle, Jim by name, jumped in to pull me out of the pool.

I should not have been so concerned since I learned my relationship with my uncle was definitely karmic. Jim had been my uncle and the husband of my current (though deceased) mother in a lifetime that was about 800 BC. At the same time, just to put a few other details into place I should note that the person who was my father in this lifetime was a guard in that incarnation. My father's karmic interaction with me in this lifetime was certainly to resolve issue coming from that lifetime. By the way, my current mother was also my mother in that incarnation, but was my wife in an incarnation of about 1400 AD.

Keeping track of karmic interactions is difficult—not so much for me or for you regarding your interactions because they make perfect sense. Getting the idea or the interactions from me to you about me for you to understand just might be the hard part—but it is not really that difficult. Try to not to put too much emphasis on the person, the role, or even the time. The whole idea of following karmic interactions is the same as following the crime scene except you are not following the money, you are following the soul. Follow the soul and all is easy to understand. Follow the soul and you can't go wrong because every reason you reincarnate is soul oriented.

Chapter Three

The other mention was my future spouse. In this lifetime I am gay, not a surprise to me and it should not be for you either. Everyone gets to be gay in at least one incarnation—you need the experience. However, you often have to wait eons before the conditions are right that will allow you to be gay, and to experience the association in the right conditions. The right amount of acceptance, the right amount of difficulty, or the right amount of anything. I chuckle whenever I hear some of the Bible thumpers going at it knowing just how wrong the Bible thumpers are. But "it's in the Bible" they yell and thump. I'm mentally going "so what?" Is there something significant in what you say? Probably not so I let it go. The right forum will be there, even if not at that moment.

My first knowledge of my spouse in this lifetime was given me at my age 15, his age 2, approximately. The detail, the information would normally have been given me at the moment of his birth, but candidly, I don't believe at age 13 I would have understood the concept of sexuality—I did not have so much trouble with it at age 15 as by then I knew I would be gay in this lifetime. Yes, I did kick the ground and cry out "why do I have to be queer, God?" but I also realized the nature of my eternity and the concept quickly became comfortable for me.

My biggest issues were thinking that my classmates might think me gay and bringing on the ridicule associated with that knowledge. Having the power of the internet and the ability to find and speak to people years after being associated with them has allowed me to learn that that they knew I was gay—even though I tried to hide it. A couple of people I looked up have mentioned the fact, but for most part it is just not an issue for people. I'll toss more in about that person revealed as my spouse at his age two as we go along. It took 49 years for me to actually see my spouse, but God updated me often enough to give me confidence and hope that we would actually be together. By the way, it was a vision—the sight of what was to come, and the detail and time too that showed me the image of my spouse, his face as he was to be when we met and a couple of distinctive physical characteristics too.

Suddenly you just know it's there when a vision comes—like a package delivered directly to your head, wrapping and all. It is a wonderful gift and I can only thank God for allowing me that gift this trip on Earth. I'll relate several stories originating with visions here—they are quite remarkable.

If you are able to climb over the obstacles put before you, then you are climbing the path of spiritual advancement. For me this lifetime, nothing seems to come easy, so I work harder. I work intelligently, and I forge ahead. It is not a ruthless endeavor, it is a purpose and direction driven course that I know I need to do. I suppose that I've been meditating all of my life—as I lay in my bed at age nine I recall the experiences I used to have. I always liked seeing the purple light gather from all sides of my sight and just go forward to oblivion. Now, I take specific steps to meditate and the same results happen—usually with a bit more to experience too—but the basic element is still there. We are creatures of God—not of a religious God—but of the creator. God is our Father—our Mother—and the salvation for all time. It is unfortunate that we don't realize all that we need to realize when thinking of God. We are faced with obstacles and we too often seek revenge, getting even, or making things right as we perceive they should be.

I do take the good advice of others, and kindly acknowledge even the unneeded, useless, and unwanted. I've often used the phrase "thank you for your opinion" when anything else would be offensive to the giver. The phrase simply says that I hear you—but commits nothing of me to use what you shared. I'll ask God for direction and consider what you provided. For all I know after all, is that what you gave me is what God gave you to give to me.

Always listen for the Voice of God in what is told you but know most is not, and some even is intended to lead you astray. Those that seek to lead you astray are persons I do avoid with appropriate fervor. Unfortunately, you cannot always avoid those persons—they come with smiles on their faces and deceit in their hearts. I'll be telling you about a person—a gifted psychic—who came with just exactly that purpose.

Well, the image of my future spouse was comforting. It is not so much what a person looks like in any given incarnation that is important but rather the connection with the soul that is important. When I saw my future spouse, I was comforted with the knowledge that he would be there in the future for me. What I did in the interim was to go about God's work knowing that this life was going to be a bit different for me.

For one, I'm doing double karma. We are all faced with obstacles in every lifetime but do double and you get to get twice the problem in only once the time. Am I sure I'm doing double karma? Better believe it. I stood before Metatron and sheepishly told Metatron that I was incarnate, gay, and doing double karma. I was saying that sheepishly as I had started to speak and wanted to finish what I was saying before realizing that I'm talking to Metatron, who simply said, knows everything. My job was to listen and I'm trying to have a conversation with the Voice of the Creator. That's OK, God is a gracious Host, and the only embarrassment I suffered was that which I inflicted on myself.

Doing double karma is a tough road to hoe, they say. In reality, you do double karma because you have become adept enough at the necessary skills to survive the challenge of more than most can handle. How do you react? Are you mad and vengeful when something does not go your way?

No, you try to determine why that was the case, and try your next feat with knowledge that failure is education—probably unappreciated education, but education none the less.

Of karma, souls are known to reincarnate in groups. The associations, the opportunity to resolve issues are all part of that. Whether it is what will become a family group, is a family group, or are persons in a given area, chances are that you knew many of them in a prior life.

I returned to Kingsport, Tennessee in 1987 where I remained until the very latter part of 1989—roughly two and a half years. The reason was economic—a failed business in Sarasota, Florida left me without options for employment in that tourist area for my industry prone skills. So, back to the place of my birth it was, and the ability to live in a trailer on the property of my father and near my grandmother. During that period, it appeared that I was going to stay in the area for a while— I've always moved often enough during my lifetime though I have come to learn why that is the case.

I always went somewhere as opposed to defaulting by chance somewhere. East Tennessee seemed good enough, but as I grew more familiar with the area and more familiar with people, one thing became very, very clear: I knew a lot of these people, though I had never set eyes on them, at least not in this lifetime.

Because of the fact that my immediate family had moved to Philadelphia, then shortly thereafter to Bucks County, Pennsylvania when I was only two to three years of age, my occasional visits for family vacation (and the mandatory visits to relatives of course), I had never met many of the people who lived in the area. Unlike their associations, I did not attend the same church, I did not attend the same schools, and I had not grown up with the same neighbors living down the street. I just did not know anyone really beyond the next door neighbor to my grandmother's home.

This period in East Tennessee gave me an unexpected opportunity to recognize people with fresh eyes—to see them from the perspective they lacked because of life-long familiarity.

Employment in the area was sparse when I moved there. I had worked for the Mason and Dixon Lines in Philadelphia, which was headquartered in Kingsport, Tennessee, but following deregulation of the transportation industry in the early 70's, the finer trucking companies lost market share to lone wolves willing to work for just the monthly truck payment. Mason and Dixon was a company that offered full services both to the industrial consumer and the expected benefits for the professional driver. They were a class act and participated in annual Truck Rodeos for professional drivers under the auspices of the American Trucking Association.

My work was not found easily—previously a police dispatcher for the local police department, a billing clerk, loader, city dispatcher and road dispatcher for Mason and Dixon in Philadelphia, even a broad range of international services learned with an international air freight company in Delaware County, Pennsylvania, just up the road (and down the taxes) from the Philadelphia Airport. I learned rating, routing, consolidation, international banking and consular work, and then entered field sales. Aside from the field sales, I was remarkable. As to the field sales, over the years I've learned that I cannot sell myself out of a paper bag. It did not matter that much anyway, this was not the area for endeavors of this kind—yes, there was the Tennessee Eastman Company, a chemical division of the Kodak Company, but I just didn't have the connections necessary to get a job in the sprawling plant. I did though socialize and I did work in a couple of local businesses.

One of those businesses was the Chicago Dough Company. I felt like a fish out of water but it was money. Not much money, but I had to buy gas and I had to buy food and the necessities of life. What I learned there was the more enlightening part of my return to Kingsport though.

Nearing the end of a day's labor at Chicago Dough Company, I was working in the kitchen when a group of other employees were leaving through the back door to the employee parking area. I had met this group at work, of course, and they were friendly and outgoing and always included me in the conversation and conviviality. What happened at that exact moment was the most intense of feelings—almost on cue, as I was in the kitchen and they leaving, they all stopped and looked at me before they left. They waited for my signal to go—it seemed as if it all had happened before and I later learned that it had. In meditation, I learned that I had worked as a Persian cook about 400 BC in Plato's household in Greece.

During that incarnation I gained well in spiritual advancement primarily as the result of aiding and assisting a group of slaves to escape, knowing that had they stayed they may well have been killed. Had I been discovered as the person assisting them, I certainly would be the person executed for the act.

There was a secret exit from the kitchen in Plato's home, I knew of it, and apparently Plato did not. That was the escape route that saved a number of souls. Those same souls were back this lifetime. I was a Persian slave then, cooking and it was my direction that saved them.

To note, the cooking has remained as an interest too. I may not be gourmet, but I carry the basic talent, enjoy great presentation and a variety of foods, and I have a philosophical bent most probably a result of being in that very famous household.

As each lifetime unfolds, we gain in talent and experience and often exhibit those same talents in subsequent incarnations.

There too was the person at a gay bar in Johnson City. Somehow I fit in well there, being almost immediately accepted.

This one tall person, about my age, drew me to him in a most remarkable way. No, it was not a sexual attraction, he a Sagittarius and I a Taurus, but I was almost like his caretaker, set to rub his back whenever I was near. In several random places around the general area, I ran into him. Without hesitation or regret I would walk up and just rub his back. I was familiar, he usually standoffish for almost everyone but I was the obvious exception. I could walk up and rub his back and he would not even have to turn his head to allow me to continue. Have someone else do the same thing though and it was as if the junk yard dog had been awakened. I knew my privileged place in this dance of old friends, and I enjoyed it.

There was strange aspect though and it was that I never even got to know much about him. Couldn't tell you what city he lived in (this is the Tri-Cities area and consisted of Kingsport, Bristol, and Johnson City in addition to many communities that dot the area) and unfortunately I cannot recall his first name. I do tend to remember astrological signs for people for some odd reason, so there the Sagittarius. But other than being a tall (at least 6'4") and lanky person, brown eyes, and brown hair and a nice smile, I cannot recall much.

I left Kingsport after two and half years for Miami. Growing up in Philadelphia just made the thought of living in such a closed thinking area more than I could bear. This area is exceptionally religiously oriented, and I was like a fish out of water. During that period in Kingsport though I had a number of remarkable psychic experiences.

Chapter Four

I spent the summer of 1986 in Sarasota, Florida at the urging of my cousin, Sherry. Sherry had a bar in Sarasota, claimed that it was a money machine, and that due to the efforts of some of her clients and a raid by the Sarasota Police Department, the place was closed down and the beer license suspended.

I had a few dollars in my pocket, I had just sold my home in Wilmington, Delaware following the rebuild from the fire and the place could be in no better shape. Practically new, the house was a showstopper just because the siding, a new door, and multiple areas of trim were upgraded with current color and current code.

My furnace fire had burned in the center of the house from the laundry/ furnace room that sat downstairs in this bi-level home, fueling the destruction of the kitchen, master bedroom and the bathroom which sat pretty well directly above the furnace.

It was a gas furnace, and it appeared that somehow the gas line had leaked or ruptured but a natural gas leak caused the house to suffer considerable damage.

It was a surreal experience. I was at Twelve Step meeting when I heard the sirens go off, and had a tinge of a premonition but I swept that premonition away and occupied myself with other concerns. I was just a mile or so from home when I felt the tinge of what was to come.

The event started a strange course of events. I returned home to find the interior of my home gutted—contents either destroyed or coated in what seemed an impermeable layer of black soot and grime. That cold January night set me on two years of rebuilding and in sheer desperation, I finally said "I've never needed you much, but God, I need you now." Perhaps that moment of desperation wasn't what really set me off on a new quest, but there was that point that reminded me that I did need God in my life. Nothing was said about religion, mind you, I really wanted God in my life.

My dog, Rusty, had managed to escape the burning house, and the neighbors were kind enough to take him in until I came home. There was a strange eeriness about the house when I pulled up—it was dark, very, very dark and a quiet that was uncomfortable and unnatural. It was winter and other than the street lights you probably would not have thought much about it but the house had a lifelessness about it that was hard to describe.

When I exited the car, I noticed that there was frozen ice on the drive way and I wondered if simply hadn't noticed it. It was frigid and it was early January 1985. The total darkness make me think that maybe there had been an electrical outage. As I climbed the stairs to the front door a car pulled up to the curb and I pushed open the door finding it unlocked and slightly ajar. Someone came up behind me.

The person was someone from the fire department who explained to me that there had been a fire. Apparently there was a short but intense fire on the downstairs level apparently fueled by escaping natural gas. The downstairs was severely damaged and the fire had burned through the floor above destroying the kitchen, a bath, while causing damage in the rest of the house with smoke and water.
I was grateful for what was saved, but truthfully little remained that I could even make use of at least until cleaned of the sooty grime. Rusty was safe and I felt good about that.

Chapter Five

Rusty was a Sheltie, a miniature collie, who surprised me one afternoon in January 1979. Near to where I lived in Wilmington, Delaware was the Concord Mall—a fairly large mall and convenient for my easy access on the weekends. Concord Mall though was more local than some of the regional malls but had all the prerequisite anchor stores and a decent selection of smaller stores.

One of those smaller stores was Doctor's Pet Center. The surprise came one afternoon about three weeks before I was to close on my first home in Wilmington. I wasn't permitted pets where I lived—a nice apartment complex with great wooded views off of Silverside Road near Philadelphia Pike in Wilmington, not too far from the Naamans Road exit of I-95 which is also the first exit into Delaware coming from Pennsylvania. When I went to shop at the mall that afternoon, a very strange thing happened.

As I entered the mall, a voice in my head yelled out "Rusty!" and did so loudly enough that if the sound could have been heard by others, then the entire mall would have heard it. It was a total shock. I had never previously gotten such a loud voice in my head. Most voices have been quiet even-metered comments or words. This time the loud shout surprised me. The voice came with such force I looked around me to see what might have prompted what sounded more like a warning to me than anything else—but there was nothing.

I was standing in a short hall entry from the parking lot to the mall and people passed left and right of me as they always do, but they were unaware of the shouting voice I had heard. Regaining my composure, I saw was that I was almost in front of a Doctors Pet Center. I had a strong and compelling need to step into the store and did that with just two or three long strides. When you are compelled from the "other side" as we all are from time to time, you are "pushed," sometimes even shoved, in a physical direction.

The drive from the other side can also be a drive by mental urge, and if you fail to do as the other side has urged, know that there will be a new type of uncomfortable for you. There is a feeling that says "You didn't do as we said, and therefore you suffer this pain." It is not pain as if you hurt your finger or stubbed your toe. This is an uneasiness that you can't shake and if you have experienced it often enough to be able to easily recognize it, then you might even set to meditation to rid yourself of the discomfort, and with a bit of luck, perhaps even understand why the "other side" has chosen to smite you.

I stepped into the Pet Center immediately—it was not my destination or intent when I arrived at the mall. There had been no reason to go there and don't recall even when or if I might have been there before. I was rushed to walk down the row of pet cages each harboring the new offspring of a pedigree breed. So young these all were that size, color, breed characteristics were hard to distinguish as I moved one cage to another. Most of the animals looked at me listlessly, perhaps one or two even hopefully that they might have a few moments of attention from the flow of anonymous and unfamiliar faces that stepped past. The urge pushed me a bit—I knew when I had to stop—it was that cage.

There was that little ball of fur in the corner, and I knew that I had to see that little ball of fur. I asked a store clerk to step near me and when she did, I asked for assistance. I wanted to hold that little ball of fur. The clerk went about her normal steps, slowly opening the cage and gently reaching in to pick up the infant dog. You could not see the dog's face, he was asleep and curled into a tight little ball and seemed unmoving. The clerk carefully cupped the small animal in two hands and nothing seemed to happen. Then though, the clerk handed the little bundle of a dog to me and as if somehow magic had happened, the small, small dog came to life in a manner that had me hooked.

The little ball of fur went for my face without the slightest hint of fear or hesitation. He was only eight weeks old but it seemed that his life purpose was to lick my face. Yes, the little thing had come alive in a manner that evoked a sudden live-giving event. Tongue licking, legs flying in all directions, he was just adorable. I asked the clerk if the store could hold the small puppy overnight while I considered purchase—it wasn't the expense frankly, but I wasn't allowed to have an animal in my rental apartment and my house purchase was still about six weeks out.

The Pet Center accepted a deposit, and I went on my way. It was only a short time later that I found myself just about home and firmly convinced that I had to have that dog. As soon as I arrived back home, I called the store and let them know that I coming right to the mall. Rules or no rules, house or no house, I had to have that puppy and I had to have it today. Of course, I did pick up the darling little Sheltie, his name was of course Rusty as the other side had so dutifully informed me, and he was my faithful companion. The amazing thing that I have learned is that he was special in even more ways.

Souls can incarnate in the bodies of animals, and other things too if you subscribe to the readings of Edgar Cayce. What is significant here is that I have become more open to being psychic, and as a result my psychic bent has opened my up to more understanding. Yes, Rusty had a soul—some soul that saw this time with me as the best opportunity for whatever its purpose was to be. Did the soul in Rusty enter to provide me just companionship during rough times in my life, or to bring out of me a caring that I did not know existed? Whatever the purpose was, or who previously I may have known as that same soul, the end was the most confirming of all the actions of that adorable dog.

In 1988, I was back in East Tennessee of course, and Rusty had been faithfully there all the way through the job I lost in 1984, the house fire in 1985 that both freed me of some things but tied me to the rebuilding and survival needed to rebuild, and being nearly new again, to sell that house. In Tennessee, I planned an evening out with friends and left my faithful companion with my father for care. When I returned home the next morning, I learned that Rusty had been let out and was apparently hit by a car. My companion of eight and a half years was dead. My father had already buried the body on a small piece of land just across the road from the house. I was heartbroken and because of what already had been done, I was without the opportunity to even see the body of my faithful friend. I stifled my feelings—they were nuisances in this awkward situation, and I just resigned myself to go about my daily business. The best thing though that happened was about a week later. There were two significant attributes that Rusty had—a familiar "thump, thump, thump" as he scratched behind his ear, and the faint "ching" as his tags touched a hard surface. It was while I sat at a desk that I head the "thump" and I heard the "ching" and I too felt the presence of Rusty. It was only for an instant heard the noise and felt the soul of Rusty, but a compelling instant that let me cry. Finally my emotion was let go and the good cry at the end set me so much better with myself and so much more accepting of the passing of my buddy.

It was not the last I saw of Rusty though and I'm reminded that soul is eternal. It was during meditation perhaps four years later that as I reached a deeper and deeper meditative state, climbing slowly up the seven layers of darkness that suddenly emerging totally around my mental range of vision a light appeared. The light coalesced in the center of the field of vision, and it was the face of Rusty—smiling, greeting, sudden.

Accompanying Rusty's appearance was his scent—another sense activated by this event. It is funny what we remember, and when the other side wants to reach us, what may be thought as insignificant can often provide the key. I haven't seen Rusty again since then perhaps because I thanked him for visiting, and realizing that my grief could hold Rusty earthbound, I thanked him, and told him that I could go on without his help if he chose to move on. I hope Rusty has moved on—I have gone on without him as best as I could. I'll only know Rusty's soul by name or relationship once I return to the other side to prepare for another incarnation. I'm looking forward to my return to the other side this time if only to understand more of the many different experiences I have seen, felt, known, and expect in this lifetime.

Chapter Six

On September 10,1987 I was scheduled for a bankruptcy hearing in Sarasota, Florida. The hearing was the end result of a year of sheer horror and absolute challenge of owning a biker bar in Sarasota. Perhaps too naïve, and particularly so when dealing with my cousin, I bought a bar from her in May 1986, a well known beer and wine bar with a built in clientele-the local biker club. What an experience! They say God only gives you what you can handle and this was one of those great experiences I suppose, as it presented more challenges than I ever expected, and at the same time provided experiences beyond normal expectation.

The bar itself was a challenge but I don't want to forget that the focus of this book is on psychic experience, so let me just jump to discussion of an experience with one of my employees. Her name was Shelly—a nice girl, an Aquarian and a pleasant looking girl. Shelly was familiar with but not deeply involved in the biker culture I believe. I've never really had anything to sway my opinion one way or the other but the clientele knew Shelly, and she just loved fitting into the raucous that rang in the bar. Between pool shots, the clatter of the balls falling in unison as each challenge between players began, the banging on the bar and tables when the cult favorite "Magic Carpet Ride" by Steppenwolf rang out—and time after time it did ring out—slamming doors, and what-have-you. It was bar and a biker bar after all. I somehow escaped the same cut as the rest—college educated and from a nice home in Bucks County, Pennsylvania, and not a tattoo to be found.

Standing a short 5'6" relative to some of the hulking people who came in, but I was the bar owner. Being the bar owner set me into the stratosphere. No one would touch me, or even try to intimate me. It is just the respect shown a bar owner. In a biker bar respect for the owner is practically a religion. Shelly fit into that scene, but I still really don't know how that happened.

Shelly was working one day before the late afternoon rush began—even bikers put in a hard day's work and my clientele in Sarasota came from all walks and from all areas in the region. But if it was the right day of the week—the week grew from a low on Monday to a near riot on Saturday—then there were several girls working. At this time in 1986-1987 the short, shorts they called "Daisy Dukes" were popular and they were short. Hiring girls for the bartending staff kept the often "not in a relationship" bikers happy with the place.

Shelly was behind the bar stocking coolers with beer—we carried several brands but everyone drank longneck Budweiser bottles. The beer was important, but Budweiser sure had a winner in that longneck bottle—everyone loved them and even though a number of the glass bottles broke, it was an incentive that moved a great number of bottles. I had my own duties as owner of course, and one was to audit the till and some other items. As I worked behind the bar as Shelly stocked, a blast of white light emanated from Shelly over a distance of about four feet, knocking me firmly backward and causing everything to go black.

Shelly turned as she heard me stumble backward against the wall but she did not realize that the energy that shot from her was even there-I slumped against the wall, trying to regain my balance but a cautious fall to the floor is all that I could manage. Shelly was unaware, I was unhurt but incredibly stunned by the charge, and neither of us ever did understand why the event occurred. It was not static electricity, it was far too powerful for that, besides the fact that there were rubber mats on the floor behind the bar. It was like lightening and I was the only one affected and I was the only one that had seen it.

The season in Sarasota, even for a biker bar, puts all of your eggs into a basket that runs generally from December to late April and since the bar that I had purchased had previously been closed, the throngs I expected never materialized and I had to close the business at the end of the first year. Cash flow stopped and all the work I had done, and all the efforts some family members made on my behalf in the form of working vacations was lost. I was driven to bankruptcy—the doors closed at the end of May and I was back in East Tennessee needing a place to live.

The legal steps that I needed to resolve took a few months, but there was a hearing scheduled on my bankruptcy on 10 September 1987. I felt that I had to go through a bankruptcy as there was to be a balloon payment at the end of the first year, and there was simply no money to accomplish that obligation.

My return to Sarasota that September landed me in Tampa, Florida, a short one hour or so ride from Sarasota. I landed, picked up my reserved car at the Tampa airport, and noticed the La Quinta Inn nearby where I had reserved a room for later that evening on my way back. I wanted to make sure that my day ended close to the airport since a mid-morning flight for the next day was reserved and it is easier to make up a late start—should that happen—when you are close rather than some distance away. Besides, I thought my visit to Sarasota would be both short and routine.

I usually plan my trips well enough that I have time to get through all of the steps I need with little problems—this trip was planned to be just the same. The drive to Sarasota was uneventful—time enough even for a quick breakfast on the way before arriving a half hour early at the Sarasota Court House in downtown Sarasota. Sarasota covers a good area and it is a lovely, wealthy, cultured town on the West Coast of Florida and it enjoys the soft waves and warm water of the Gulf of Mexico. Just noting too, but like Lancaster, Pennsylvania, there is a heavy Amish presence. My understanding is that these people came from groups in Ohio, but I'm relating chatter, not research fact.

I met my attorney outside of the courtroom and we reviewed notes and signed some papers, and after a short hearing, I had finally been able to stop this failed business. A biker bar is a wealth of experience and the overall takeaway left me a more confident and seasoned person. Me, at my 5'6" and about 150 pounds, could stand up to, and be compassionate and understanding to, a drunken guy in chains, leather, and symbols—most of which conveyed something related to death, fear, or mayhem, and who wore boots built to stomp a head or touch a roadway all in a day's duty. Often enough, I had the inclination to run but it was my business, it was my responsibility, and it was my call so I sucked it up and did what was necessary. The stress that I had was relieved when the bankruptcy was finalized and I at last felt like a free man.

It had been several months since I had been in Sarasota and before coming down I tried to line up a few friends to see. Being away for even that amount of time let's you see the number of things that change. People move, the old familiar is no longer the old familiar, and suddenly I felt like the outsider. I did manage though before I came down to speak with a friend, David, who was too ill to see me. He had contracted AIDs and in that time, AIDs was still the death sentence for almost everyone who contracted the disease. It was only three years after the first time that I became aware of the disease, which was in 1984 if memory serves me right. David sounded ill, he sounded weak, but he was still a friendly person. I had hired David's brother Chris, a young man to come into the bar every morning and clean up—the general morning after cleaning that is necessary for a business like a bar, and Chris had introduced me to his brother, David.

This time David wanted to let me know about someone he had met. That person was a psychic, he said, and "she knows everything about you" just as soon as you do meet. That person was Geneva Sapp. David gave me her phone number and suggested that I call her.

It was getting sometime in the mid afternoon when I called Geneva—and she stopped for a moment before telling me that "yes, she would see me." I didn't realize exactly how much I had lucked out, but apparently I won the jackpot.

Geneva Sapp was indeed a very special person—and even as I write this I'm getting the feeling that she might be close. I do suspect that she has "passed over" but I've not been able to confirm anything for quite a long time. I met Geneva on 10 September 1987, and the year now is 2012, and Geneva was already of advanced age at our first meeting—she would be very, very old if another 25 years were tacked onto her life. We all live the life we are supposed to—very few live to the late 90's or 100's so I'm going to assume she is gone now.

Geneva Sapp is (or was) the psychic consulted by the Sarasota Police Department. As I arrived at her home, I learned this detail as she was then meeting with a couple of people from the department, and I sat quietly in her living room as she completed her conversation. As that business finished, her guests departed and I recall overhearing some things that can only be described as perplexing.

Geneva saw and the persons from the Police Department agreed that certain things were going to happen, but since those things had not yet happened, there was no action that could be taken. Our justice system does provide that a person is innocent until proven guilty, and even more so, if an event has not transpired, no action could be taken. From the psychic perspective, conspiracy is not the problem when you can see the end, but you still have to wait for an act to be able to act on it. The department's hands are tied until the event occurs. Tired from her work though, Geneva turned to me her guests just now departed.

Geneva was the epitome of the kindly grandmother, and she was an African-American with hair streaked with gray. Soft spoken, she conveyed a warm, wonderful presence that belied her ability and impact on my life.

I politely introduced myself, and Geneva asked me to sit for a few minutes while she gathered herself and apparently allowed herself to recuperate from her prior psychic work. From my own current experience, channeling can be exhaustive, pulling both an energy stream through you and robbing you of your energy at the same time. Your energy is a very real thing—it can be added to, and quickly exhausted even by the mere contact with a person who is capable of robbing energy, and there are many persons who fall into that category.

Sometimes you only learn of them when it is too late—I've lost enough energy often enough and usually by total surprise. When in a high energy state, it might just be better to stay from everyone, period.

Geneva had me sit down on a sofa and relax while she set up a small cassette recorder—a real blessing since it never even occurred to me to record the reading. I barely knew then what a reading was, but I have learned so much more since then, and there are new things to learn all the time. Just encounter a new objective, try a new approach, and suddenly a whole new set of "psychic rules" pop up to confuse and interfere with your objectives.

Geneva finally sat down and leaned back slightly. She seemed to take on a different appearance—she gently rocked back and forth in her seat and as she opened her mouth and the first word was uttered, I surprised myself by immediately breaking out in tears.

During the total of two hours during which Geneva gave me my reading, I cried. It was not my intent to cry, but it was the most wonderful cleansing I can every recall. Tears streamed from my face—I felt as if I were standing before God while Geneva spoke, and I was here to admit to all the things wrong in my life. I had to say almost nothing, but every word from Geneva seemed to open a chapter that I had slammed shut long, long ago. I looked at what I should have been doing, and what I was doing. I looked at how I handled people, and how I should have handled people. I considered the challenges I did not want to face and then considered how I was going to face them anyway. This was not a reading to know my future, it was a reading to put God's will into context of my present, and into the past of this life. I was overwhelmingly terrified—not of Geneva nor even of God's will, but of the many things I was to have done in this life that I had brushed aside or declined to do.

This life was here, this life was now, and this life is the one that I had to deal with and the sooner that I deal with it, the better. Somehow the reading came to an end nearly two hours later and I realized what an extreme weight bore on me now. Geneva had said that she was tired when we began but I knew she rose to the occasion anyway. I was embarrassed by the disclosure of my life to a stranger, confused by all that I had experienced, and anxious about what I should do next. I thought my meeting with Geneva would be a walk through the park—I never dreamed that this event—this meeting—would have such an impact on me. I gathered myself and asked Geneva what I owed her.

Suddenly I felt that our agreed price was far too little, but at the same time I had no extra money to give. I quickly passed Geneva her fee in folded dollars and prepared to leave. Still, Geneva was kind and supportive and made sure that I had her phone number—I was allowed to contact her again if I liked. I was so confused then that I didn't really know what I wanted, but I thanked her again and quietly left her home.

The ride back to Tampa was quiet for most part—Tampa is only about an hour north of Sarasota and I didn't even turn on the radio. No, I continued to cry and as I did cry, I prayed out loud in the quiet sanctuary of the car. "What have I done and how can I fix it, Lord?", I cried over and over. It was not what Geneva said that I wondered about, no, it was that her words threw open doors and I feared looking into those closets, those caves where my darkest secrets lived. I know now that it is not the deed that is such a problem, but our failure to address the issues that we agreed to long before our birth. I had experienced the same life review with my eyes wide open that we all get once we have passed from this earth. The understanding is wrenching and the burden profound.

We all have a contract with God—executed well before we are born and the better we address those obligations the better we'll succeed in this life. Is what we perceive as that scale that is important to gauge our success? No, if wealth accumulation is that what we say shows our success, can we really be successful knowing of the wealth accumulated by Bill Gates of Microsoft? In that comparison, we've already lost the race—we have failed in accumulating that sum.

That is not the test—the test is whether we have worked, whether we have taken the opportunities and the chances that God has presented to us. Have we held faith, and more importantly trust, in God and the expectation that he will help us? Have we held that trust in greater stead than we have embraced the fear that we'll be left alone, without God's help and input? As you wake each day, affirm your reliance on God simply by asking "Lord, what will you have me do today?" Start your life always that way, and the benefits flow, the understanding emerges, and the opportunities present themselves. Little by little, bit by bit, you turn to your Creator for the guidance and relief and soon come to expect, to find, and to use those opportunities presented to you.

Crying all the way back to Tampa and having cried all during the two hours of Geneva's reading, I was exhausted and quickly checked into the La Quinta Inn near the airport where I had made reservations. Fortunately for me, a nearby restaurant was open and I went there for a small salad—I wasn't really hungry but it had been hours since I had eaten and even though I did not want to speak to anyone, it seems comforting at least to be somewhere with others. After a brief time, I left the restaurant for the comfort of my room.

Chapter Seven

Like most hotel rooms, this one was just fine. Well appointed, clean, neat, and my sanctuary for the evening, and chosen as it was convenient to the airport for my trip back to Tennessee the next morning.

My mood was still the same—in my mind I churned all that happened that day, a bankruptcy hearing, searching for friends and finding none as it seemed everyone had moved on, then a dramatic reading by a person who could see into my soul. I stood in front of the mirror at the desk in the motel room. I questioned myself some more and as I did the tears streamed from my eyes. I felt ripped apart, vulnerable and abused, but injuries of my own making. There was no one else to blame and I didn't try to do so knowing that everything, from the contract with God to my failure to complete that contract was of my own. I take my own responsibilities—it is very important to do so. Know your own weight and carry it. Where to go from here, I wondered?

I looked deeply into my own eyes—red and watered from tears and confusion. It was a simple mirror over the desk—every motel has that same mirror I believe, and it is probably the requisite item besides a bed that qualifies a room to be called a motel room. The La Quinta Inn was well-appointed and bright as I had hoped, now illuminated with lamps as it was late but fatigue was creeping in as the mind continued to race. The start of a course of events that has changed my life began without warning, without preparation, and without understanding.
Looking into my own eyes, I realized that the image in the mirror changed. My same eyes, but the head, the face I had known since birth now was different. I was looking at a man's head that was larger, familiar, and in some strange way terrifying!

"What was happening", I wondered as shock made me feel that my whole world was changing. My footing in reality seemed lost. Quickly, that image faded and another image replaced that image in the mirror. Again, the eyes were the same but the head was different and I noticed that I could see the gentle slope of the neck and upper torso. That image too faded quickly and another image of a man appeared, and I saw that in addition to all that I was already noticing that there was a quality, a glow, that also applied to the images.

Then I realized that a whole progression of images was emerging and as I looked in awe I kept my eyes focused on the very same eyes I had seen before the changes began. They were my eyes, each image bore my eyes. One after another, a slow change but a definite change was occurring and as I remained fixated on the mirror, I began to dance around in front of the mirror with an excitement I did not understand. Suddenly clarity came to my thoughts and I realized that "these images are all of me! Each face, each image, each nose, each cheek—they are all mine! The images I see are me!

Just as I regained enough composure to breath, one image stopped and lingered. That image, a man in his late 20's to mid 30's with auburn hair in a Prince Valiant cut—bangs and long hair with upturned ends, lingered. Then, from what looked like what should have been a finger on the back of the mirror, an "X" started to be drawn. From upper left to lower right, upper right to lower left, an "X" covered the face and I realized that single lifetime had ended in suicide, my suicide. A cold sense enveloped me and I felt great pangs of loneliness. In that lifetime, I had thrown God's gift back to him—rejecting the greatest opportunity a soul can be given. In a moment though, the progression of images continued and lifetime after lifetime presented the face I had worn for the world to see. Near the end of the experience, I could still see me, but there was no face, no body, associated with the radiance in the mirror. No, I was just God's creation, a soul on the earth plane. I felt myself to be a crystalline entity—sheer power, sheer good, encased in nothing but the Glory of God.

I've had a long time to ponder that experience, and three things emerged that I was made aware of that are part and parcel of the information conveyed.

One, time. The span of time over which my incarnations were displayed was about ten and a half million years—give or take a bit. You feel time more than experience it in these type of experiences—you "just know" if you will and I'm sure that the skeptics will feel very, very uncomfortable with that quick brush of opinion. To that I say only that you really should just start meditating—or arrange a hypnotic regression with a hypnotherapist. Experience details of your own past lives and you'll clearly understand what happens, even if not in a form or format that would necessarily be consistent with calendars, logs, spreadsheets, or what have you.

Two, spiritual advancement. The sole soul purpose for incarnating is to advance spiritually—the effort more productive and faster on the earth plane than is available on the spirit plane. As I watched the progression of faces that was my linear heritage of incarnations, I realized that some lives had been lived better than others. The aura, that beautiful light that emanates from the soul, varied in intensity, clarity, color, and instinctively I knew that the light, bright light surrounding each image told me whether the life had been well lived, or poorly executed. My feeling of time told me that the face of the incarnation that had been exed out was from around 1400 AD. The lifetimes that followed, particularly those that felt as if they were in the middle ages, were not so well lived. They conveyed a darker appearance, a lack of progress on the earth plane. I could only imagine that the times, the society, the need to survive may have driven me to acts that were not what I would have purposely written on the "skeins of time and space" as described by Edgar Cayce, referring to the Akashic Records, the repository of all of a soul's experiences. (Edgar Cayce is thought to have derived the information that is carefully preserved in his library at the Association For Research and Enlightenment (EdgarCayce.Org) in Virginia Beach, Virginia, from the Akashic Records).

Three, age. Not every incarnation was experienced in the same definition of "lifetime." No, from the first incarnation, that crystalline entity form, to the last, that of George Herbert Leigh Mallory, lifetimes varied. The first, the soul without a body, seemed to last a long, long time—a five thousand year lifetime did not seem odd. A lifetime that long should not seem odd either, as our closeness and direct knowledge of God is what seems to prompt the longer existence on earth, while my last completed incarnation ended as it neared the 38ᵗʰ year, ended by the inadvertent plunge from the face of Mount Everest.

Other quirky details were conveyed too: from the Prince Valiant auburn hair worn at the time of my suicide to knowing that I've had white hair in seven prior lifetimes. I wear that same white hair today seen previously and I assume that I must like it as I have chosen to wear it so often.

There was one element of the experience that I must stress—the eyes are indeed the window to the soul. As the experience unfolded, the eyes carried an appearance and essence—a sameness that linked each incarnation. This understanding explains the incredible recognition we get from time to time when we meet someone whom we have known in a prior life. That ease, that familiarity, that comfort of knowing someone whose name we have yet to know in this incarnation.

As this progression displayed in the mirror in that motel room, I danced around in sheer excitement with an uncontrolled energy and when the images ended and finally faded from the mirror, I felt drained and exhausted, shocked and confused well beyond understanding. My mental state had already been emotionally ripped from the events of the day and now this had happened.

I looked around the room, found my cigarettes on a side table (smoking has long since gone by the wayside, but this was 1987 after all), and lit one up. Pulling back the chair at the desk, I slid quickly down on the seat before I fell into it. The feeling and the confusion was overwhelming, and I could not feel any more. I was not excited nor was I even capable of feeling—there was a numbness about me that prevented me from understanding exactly what was happening.
Without warning a strong rap on my right shoulder came, an overwhelming feeling again, a new and vibrant feeling, but so quickly enveloping me that I didn't have time to feel it but it still held me—removing me from my sense of association with the room around me.

I said to myself "I feel like I've been Touched by God" and suddenly as if my thoughts had taken a life of their own the phrase "Touched by God" began turning over and over in my head. I visualized the experience, seeing the form of the words spinning ever faster and faster. My right hand was still holding a cigarette while I tried to glance to see where the ashtray was—at fingertip length fortunately and I set the cigarette down thinking I was going to lose consciousness and fearful of setting the room on fire had the cigarette fallen to the carpeted floor.

What a strange thought that was—at a time when the Universe seemed to be changing around me. The phrase continued over and over, faster and faster: "Touched by God, Touched by God, Touched by God, Touched by God" and my sense of presence changed and I felt myself suddenly being drawn into a vortex, a tunnel, likely the tunnel so often quoted by those passing from this life to the next but fortunate enough to return.

Was my body being drawn in, I wondered? I could not tell but as I was being drawn somehow and it was that tunnel that I was experiencing— the walls were lined with faces, many, many faces and I passed them quickly, and then even more quickly, and as the experience continued streaks of light passed by me, or perhaps me by them, but I had still that sense of moving. There was the distinct feeling of moving up—but I could not look back to see from where I had come and I could barely see ahead of me but I was moving.

It was terror that overcame me as I moved up the tunnel, but not the type that would have me run from the room screaming. No, this was sitting in the car on a roller coaster, holding onto the rails with dear life, only to have the rails evaporate from your touch.

Our sense of being in control keeps all of us grounded, we call it fear when we realize that we are no longer in control, and we usually panic. I was there, but with the added element of absolute astonishment and amazement. I didn't recall having ever experienced this action, this sensation but I had no choice. It seems just a moment later that the feeling subsided as I continued to move forward, to move upward, as it felt to me then. I did not experience the "white light" as all of this was occurring and I had no idea of my destination, but I soon began to relax.

To say I burst out of the tunnel would be wrong—instead I just seemed to suddenly be in a huge cavernous area where all about me, in absolute order and symmetry, other souls gathered as I was now doing. In front of me, in the center of this gallery was a plank. The plank, which seemed to have no beginning but ended exactly in the center of the gallery, had square cornered edges, and a depth that made it appear stable. The color of the plank appeared gray, the gallery blue and punctuated with the absolute white of the souls also gathered with me to observe. On the end of the plank, an orb.

The orb was a lighter gray on top, a darker color on the bottom, a perfectly round item that could be a small bowling ball or such if not for the colors and the line that divided the top from the bottom. There I observed a scalloped effect—a line that circumvented the orb in a wavy effect. On reflection, I see this as the origin of the ying and the yang depiction used in modern graphics and on everything from notebook paper to jewelry. There are many aspects of our true existence that we bring into the material world—this just a wonderful example of that true origin.

I stayed there, feeling all that was around me. There was an energy that pervaded me and like using more voltage than normal, or putting high octane fuel into an engine that usually was fueled with kerosene.

The energy was overwhelming and though I tried to stay as long as I could, I was soon overtaken by the need to leave. I felt myself pull back, and discovered that I was still sitting at the desk in that motel room, but a hole literally floating in front of me that a remaining visual gateway to the other side. I leaned forward, curious if nothing else, and put my face back into that hole. The feeling, the energy again overcame me and I had to pull back. It was just more than I could handle. As I pulled back I glanced at the now burned down cigarette in the ashtray and saw that the glow of the burning tobacco had gone, ash falling in an arc into the ashtray. Looking back to the oval to the other side, I was disappointed to see that that access was gone. My experience for that evening had come to an end.

I was exhausted. The energy of the day, the reading from Geneva, the drive and the crying, and now incredible adventure on the "other side" all added up to take the very last bit of my body's ability to continue. I reached for the light and turned it off, falling into my bed and going off to a sleep that had no dream.

Chapter Eight

I awoke refreshed if not confused by the events of the day and night before. The images from the night before were vivid and perplexing—though I knew what had happened, I did not know why it had happened—it just did. If for me not having been there, done that, I would questioned the events myself—I didn't really consider what I would say to others—there had been no contact yet with anyone else. I felt as if I were walking on eggshells as I slowly gathered my belongings and dressed for the day and the flight home.

On board the plane I sat quietly, pondering a new sense that God was always watching. "Ooops, don't want to do that wrong, what will God think of this", I wondered silently to no one in particular, but I've never been the type of person to hold secrets. Never disrespectful of the privacy of others, but still unsure what I should say to someone if they asked. "If they asked?" I thought—who even would conceive of the events that I had gone through just the night before, much less ask. What a strange and unseemly idea, I wondered again. "Ask?" No, no one would ask anything but I was bursting with the need to share this remarkable event and no one even sat near me in the plane—and in a confined space was not where I wanted to start a conversation about seeing me, in lifetime after lifetime for eons going back to the beginning. "No," no one would ask. I turned to the stewardess and started to say something, but my throat failed to make the sounds that she would understand. No words came, just a guttural sound that I quickly averted and then I sat firmly down into my airline seat. I pulled the seat belt around me and securely latched it. It was close to takeoff and I needed a change of scenery and I needed it now! The ride home was quiet with me in deep thought and my eyes seeing so much landscape but not registering a thing in my mind. I chose not to bring the story to anyone as I traveled. It was unbelievable to me—it would certainly be unbelievable to anyone else.

The event was finally shared on return to my home where I spoke candidly to my roommate, who hearing me relate the details said one thing that I have heard on two occasions now. As he looked into my eyes as any friend would, he said "you have changed." What the change was or is, I don't know. However changed, I felt it a dramatic change that I could not see from my side of the mirror. Perhaps the mirror in the motel room knew, but beyond that one evening, I don't believe the secret in the mirror will ever again be given up.

Not all of my psychic experiences are as profound as that just described, but there are many that rank right up there on the scale of incredible. There will be necessary overlaps in all the stories that I'm relating as some began in very early age and still are being played out still today, while others have run their course even though that course took nearly thirty years to play out. Let me relate the specifics of one such request placed to me by God in hopes that it brings a greater understanding to you as how associations interplay from lifetime to lifetime.

This course of events began at a very specific time on a very specific date. The time was 11:57 PM, and the date was December 25, 1979—yes Christmas day but that more coincidental than relevant. To begin, I was sitting in the kitchen of my home in Wilmington, Delaware, lonely and despairing that the day had been so uneventful. I don't recall exactly what had me so glum but it may well have been that it was Christmas day, and I had had no guests, no visitors, and had not ventured out myself. There was no friend or companion to speak to as I lived in a large home and lived there by myself. Had it not been for my dog Rusty, there would not have been another sign of life, and it was late and I had inebriated myself with alcohol as I had done for several years with very definite regularity and a total lack of control. A good buzz never made me feel better, it just stopped me from feeling. Period.

Drink enough and the world was kept at bay for a while. Sure I would wake up hung over and drawn out, but for now the future was not an issue and withdrawal from self and society provided the surest way to avoid the pain and pang of loneliness.

The kitchen window provided a glance into the back yards of the neighbors, me sitting at the bottom of a "V" with the backyards of neighbors going both left and right. All day I watched, and I drank, and no sign of life disturbed my watching. Both complacent and resigned I sat there but there was no expectation of change. It is Delaware and trees were bare and grey against the sullen sky—even the cheery Christmas lights were on the other sides of the houses away my view and I lacked wonderment and motivation to view them anyway.

If Christmas were over I wouldn't have to face up to another depressing holiday for a least a week. New Years was coming and I knew I would be drunk well before the clock struck midnight then. It was the pattern, after all.

Here came 11:57 PM—it didn't creep up on me and I was concerned about the time at all. No, had Christmas Day slipped to Boxer Day without my notice that would be just fine, thank you. I'll have another drink and if my eyes become burdensome and the eyelids cause me to slip into a slumber sitting in the kitchen, or if I make it to bed, that is fine too. Not tonight.

No, at this hour on this day the room suddenly seemed filled with a presence and there I now stood at the refrigerator reaching for a beer. I stood fully up suddenly and from wall to wall, baseboard to baseboard and fully across the ceiling the presence filled the room. Nothing to see, nothing to hear, nothing to explain why the room took on a feeling that I don't recall having ever felt before. This happened so quickly that there was not time to consider, it just was.

"Will you take care of him?" That Voice emanated from everywhere and my only inclination was to look up as I spread my arms fully outward, and without thinking, my voice answered "yes!". Unknowing as to whom I just promised to take care of I said "who?" And the Voice said "You will know." I'll know, I wondered. That's my answer, "I'll know?" "He'll need you", the exchange went on. When?, I asked, and the feeling of 30 years enveloped me, as I stammered to get "why" out of my throat. "He'll need you—drugs, alcohol, prostitution, pornography", then four more needs were said but I could barely understand much less commit the detail to memory.

"You will be reminded" I heard and I let the description move on without further question—now I was realizing that I was speaking to God. Who else, what else could it be but God? I got the feeling that I was scrambling for detail and the Voice seemed to move quickly along but I barely caught the details as this rush of thought filled my mind, my ears, and looking straight up my eyes saw nothing but the ceiling of my kitchen.

I asked where he was and the response was that he was being born—now! He was being born in Saint Louis (Missouri) but he would come from Dallas (Texas). That was all very confusing in the moment but I grabbed what I could and held onto what I could. Fortunately, I thought, I would be reminded.

The strangest thoughts came to my mind—me, a man of 31 years expecting a man being born right now to find me in thirty years. I'm not a man particularly interested in younger men. No, rather, as George Herbert Leigh Mallory, I only had two desirable options that would apply here in dealing with younger men. I'll be a teacher or I'll be a father figure—but to seek, find, or want carnal knowledge of a child is just not me. This seemed curiously interesting though. A young man who would be about half my age seeking me out some 30 years in the future would make me the envy of my of peers in the gay world. Nothing quite like having a young man as a trophy on your arm to elicit envy.

If that is what God wants, who am I to disagree? That thought was never a serious consideration, I'm too well balanced and too much aware of my personal responsibility in society. I don't try to elicit envy and I'm not playing for one-upmanship. What I have consistently strived for is to do the best possible to meet the need, and to involve everyone in achieving the best possible outcome with the best possible input. I would just wait and see what transpired with this young man, but responding to God's request was easy: take care of him? Sure! God asked and I was willing, ready, and to best of my thinking, able to do.
If this were the only thoughts in my head maybe I would have remembered this request for the thirty years that it was going to take to play out.

That was not the case, as I started to have to deal with my alcohol problem in the days, months, and years that followed. Work for me has always been fun and I was working for an international air freight company and doing quite well in my duties. All was fine there until I decided to go from the operational side of the work to the sales job. I have finally come to the realization that sales for me is not for me. Sure, I'm analytical, and I evaluate product for quality and durability, and for me, selecting the best and yet the most economical product is fine. I don't have the ability though to sell a product or service to someone else. Come to me for assistance, and you'll get the best selection too.

Let me come to you to try to have you purchase a particular product, and I don't quite get to the finish line. In sales, that is called closing and closing is the most important part of the sale. It is where you sign the dotted line, where the cash or check is taken, and where the product is set to be finally delivered. Others are far more qualified for that than I am.

My drinking led eventually to a desire to stop drinking—I could not stand the daily hangover, the vacations spent at home in total inebriation. I managed my personal life reasonably well for a drinker— perhaps as good or better than most—but the problems drinking caused never went away. My promise to God was years away so the thought needed to keep my promise there in the forefront of my mind slipped back somewhere. I had more pressing needs to consider.

Sometime in 1983 after trying to keep it together and asking the help of people in a well respected Twelve Step Program, I decided to do a stint in a rehabilitation facility. I chose Hiddenbrook Rehabilitation Center in Bel Air, Maryland.

The thirty days there finally severed the stranglehold that alcohol had on me and for the next eight months, I was sober. Life was still difficult, but at least I was not making it worse and I adopted a lifestyle free of alcohol. In May of 1984 following an argument with someone I let my anger and self importance prevail and I drank—surely it was self will run riot. The next morning, and surely as an act of providence, the counselor from the rehabilitation center called. It was incredibly the very next day—and I told them that I had "slipped" the night before. I don't recall them ever following up previously, but that day they did. I haven't heard from them since either, but the call set me on a path that has not since been diverted. I don't drink. The problem is identified, relegated to daily caution, and with the help of friends in the twelve step program, I maintain my sobriety.

I had not thought of God's request really since taking steps to make my life better. Yes, jobs are always a problem, the realities of homes, other issues that life presents to us all. Still, there were other issues that God had me working on. I have never felt removed from God. I'm just doing what I'm told, or at least what I think I'm being told.

The details here began to unfold again on the first of May 2009. A small town in Central Louisiana was my home, having left the Cruise Line in March 2006 and finally finding a buyer for my Florida town home. I learned quickly that being older is presents more challenges in securing a job and I felt some of my attempts to find work were being thwarted by efforts from my old employer, or so it seemed.

Sale of my home was necessary and I am sure that God had decided that I was to leave it, but also decided, that I would leave that home with profit in hand. Seems leaving a home at that time with profit in hand was getting more and more difficult in a declining real estate market. I had purchased my Miramar town home pre-construction and at the urging of my spirit guides. Since I had also purchased upgrades specifically for the intent of resale, I managed to escape in reasonably good shape with a profitable sale amount, and a surprisingly short time on the market.

As often I am motivated to take an action, the purchase of the town home pushed against my personal inclination but the feeling that this had to be done came from that same place where I meet God in meditation and so done it was!

The development where I bought sold every one of the 196 townhomes in one day—and lucky me, mine was waterfront at a discount!

Chapter Nine

Here I sat then in a gay bar in this central Louisiana town where I had moved thinking that it had the same warm southern hospitality normally experienced in the general area of the southern United States. This was not that place, but I was still a bit fuzzy on the idea in that I had been there only a year, and I had found employment in a local call center for one of the top four cell phone companies in the country.

I don't recall the exact time that evening but there was never much of a crowd anyway it seemed, and I seldom stay for long. My favorite drink is either ginger ale or if I feel like it, an O'Doules is great for that now forbidden taste of beer.

Problem with most of the alcohol free beers is that two is the maximum as the flavor just fades with more. Consumption is limited to two and it is time to go. I was on that second bottle of not-so-cold beer when a young man walked in, and almost like magic walked directly to me. I am a cautious person, but I was flattered by his attention and struck up a conversation anyway. His name was Bobo, he said, a nickname obviously, and I was sorry to sense that he had the smell of alcohol on his breath.

Someone arriving at a bar with alcohol on their breath was a red flag for me, someone still dealing with an alcohol problem. My then twenty five years of sobriety is dear to me, and I protect it with resolve and determination. Still, we do our best to work with the still-practicing alcoholic. I wasn't sure that Bobo was an alcoholic, but my first impression had me considering that possibility.

Over the past couple of weeks I had been in this bar more often than I usually went anywhere. I thought it just because I wanted some human interaction and was hoping to find someone to relate to. God has given me a wonderful mind and what I have found is that there are few people other than professionals that I easily relate to. Too smart, too insightful, few people "get me" if you will, though I try to be part of any group I meet, but sophomoric humor is not my style, and they seldom concern themselves with the topic of the day from CNN, even if that is all we have in common. So, I tend to keep to myself and I'll find someone to talk to somehow over time.

Bobo let it all loose just about as soon as we met. He told me he was from Dallas, he had a cell phone but the number no longer worked due to a "temporary suspension" which is code word for lack of payment. I didn't feel put on by him, and as might be expected, he had a couple more beers to add to the state of inebriation he had when he arrived. Those were on my tab, of course.

Bobo told me that he had a daughter who was with her mother, and he loved her dearly but I got the idea that he given up parental rights, and only saw his daughter on rare occasion. He also told me that he was not allowed to visit his mother in Dallas, restricted by her demand based on his abuse of rights at home. How unfortunate for a twenty nine year old not to be able to see his mother and cut off even from his daughter. There was both a brother and a sister, and the brother was cool but the sister was as critical as the mother he said. They just didn't seem to get along.

I asked, as if I really thought it would do any good, if he could get a couple of weeks of sobriety under his belt. At the end of the evening, I offered him a ride home. It was not very far that I had to drive Bobo, but he asked me to drop him off in front of an old industrial building, an office in front and a large ramshackle building attached at the rear with a stone and broken concrete parking area. Bobo said he lived here, but I couldn't see the part that even suggested that there might be a residence nearby.

I would learn the truth, but it wasn't apparent then. I figured that I would see him again at the bar, and we made no specific plans. My evening was over, and almost as soon as Bobo left the cab of my pickup, he seemed to disappear. I looked around, but I didn't know where he had gone. I left, and went home for sleep.

Sleep came easily—I had nothing on my mind and in this little Louisiana town there was not much that lingered from the day to cause me to be restless. This time, the anxiety came from a dream—a reminder from the other side that set me on a path of completing the promise I had made to God.

I dreamt about Bobo. I saw him emerging from a closet into my view and I suddenly realized from the dream that my promise made almost thirty years prior had came to fruition—it was time to do my duty to God. I saw Bobo in that dream, and I remembered the promise, and God reminded me of my association with Bobo—a soul I had known for eons before and form whom I held an incredible love.

We love the soul, not the person. The child born on Christmas years before who God asked me to take care of had arrived—and I almost didn't recognize him. God said I would be reminded—this was that time.

I didn't know where Bobo lived, or at least I didn't realize where he lived, and from time to time I drove by the industrial building where I dropped him off looking for a residence. The building always seemed locked up, and I had usually made my drive by after I finished work at the customer service call center in town. My search was confusing, so from time to time I went back to the little bar where I had met him.

At first, I just stayed and hoped that he would come in—I never bothered the staff for their assistance. After a couple of hours the wait would bore me and I would leave. As time wore on several visits later, I did ask the bartender if he had seen the person I was looking for—I even presented a single photograph from my cell phone to help. A verbal description of a person is just difficult to use to find someone.

One night a new bartender was on duty, so I posed the question and displayed the picture just hoping. The new bartender did know the person, Bobo, and said that he had been in, just not on the same nights that I related my own visits. OK, so we were off schedule, but I still wanted to find him. About that time, Bobo comes up behind me and does a friendly little head butt move. I was very pleased to finally see him—it was now the 16th of May, more than two weeks since our first meeting. I was determined not to lose track of him this time.

With the love that I had felt from the dream that occurred on the evening of our first meeting, I had a different perspective on what our relationship was going to be. I'm twice his age so I didn't really think that it would be a sexual relationship, and it was not. I'm glad it wasn't as that allowed me to keep things in perspective and emotionally objective as possible even as difficult as that was anyway. As it turns out, I never did see Bobo outside of the fog of alcohol or drugs, it would not have been fair to pursue anything other than a fatherly association.

It would have been interesting to know exactly what God wanted me to do before the relationship began, but these things tend to play themselves out. Bobo lacked the moral compass to say no to many things—instead, as evidenced by the drug use, the out-of-wedlock child, and his selection of friends, he seemed to go with the flow even if it was obvious that the flow was really a raging river of error. We all make mistakes in life, some are simply bigger mistakes than others.

Bobo had the ability to talk to the other side though I feel strongly that he was being influenced by both his guides—those who work in a person's behalf for good—and those spirits who seek to harm the earthbound for their own sadistic purposes. Bobo was influenced by both and I'm sure of that as he would on occasion warn me of impending events, but then seek to take action to pursue something absolutely negative.

I had cut off my guides early in my life, selecting instead to go the route on my own. This decision would help me achieve even more spiritual advancement if I did well and I have never forgotten that my choices had not to be correct, but rather consistent with God's dictate of love and help.

After my guides told me to tell my first grade teacher that I was George Mallory, and being immediately and firmly rejected, I was thoroughly embarrassed and recall asking them later if it was my job "to do as they say."

So far, even though failing in the material success I would enjoy, my choices are based on my desire to help and respect others. Until the final scorecard is tallied I won't know if I have done well, but I do continuously try. My guides have never failed to act in the best for my interest in the end, and along with prophesy I have received protection.

Looking back at my lifetime, it would have been nice to have the interactive conversation, and I'm still looking for the return of my guides for that benefit.

A few nights before a trip to New Orleans for the July 4th holiday in 2009 my dreams had brought a firm message: If I am requested to go to the 5th ward, do not. If I go, I will lose my life. I shared this warning with no one. That is a fairly strong message and I remembered it well. My visit to New Orleans turned out to be difficult enough. I was trying to get Bobo away from the town we lived in as he seemed to have found the source of drugs that fueled some very strange behavior. I really was not familiar with all the symptoms of drug use, especially the anxiety and agitation that results from certain drug use.

I had made reservations at what has become my favorite motel chain, La Quinta, and I looked forward to a night's good rest. We had two queen sized beds in the room and Bobo fidgeted while watching television. I had driven some four hours with this person who insisted on stopping for beer too many times, who had insisted on having the music in the car as loud as could be accomplished, even prompting my beloved Sheltie Sara to attempt to leap through the drivers window of my moving car. Bobo was a problem to say the least.

Pulling the covers over my head, I managed a fretful fall to sleep. It seemed only a short time later that Bobo was over nudging me to wake up but a glance at the clock told me that it was already past midnight. He asked me to take him to the 5th ward, and I replied no, thinking about the warning given me from the other side. Huffing anger, Bobo left the room. I had saved myself and I was pleased. When Bobo came back a couple of hours later, he was finally ready for sleep and I learned that he had spent his time at a nearby Denny's, a restaurant that was open all night. He had made no trip to the 5th ward—wherever that might have been. God had asked me to take care of him and I'm grateful that I was getting help for the endeavor.

Back in Central Louisiana I dropped Bobo off the next day and I didn't see him for several days. I usually tried to stop by where he lived but as often as not, he would deny me entry unless he had no money for food, in which case I was welcome as long as I took him somewhere for food. If he had money, he would buy something as work ended and pick up cans of beer but if I came by he would open his door, see me, then just slam the door and that meant that I was not welcome. His residence was surprising—in exchange for payment devoid of taxes, his employer, a small kitchen cabinet manufacturer and installer, he could live in an interior room in this workshop area, and pay nothing for utilities. At least that was the arrangement he told me, and absolute truth was not the foremost concern in Bobo's mind. His drug use and attempts at rationalization were paramount. I knew who he was and I willingly ignored such affronts to do God's will. Bobo never seemed to get our connection—at least not during his life. Bobo had gotten himself not only into a personal hell with drugs, he had stumbled into a very strange local custom.

This little town in Central Louisiana is the only place I have ever encountered that actually has orgies as part of the local scene. Oh, they try to be discrete about it, but live in the area long enough, encounter the events, and everyone eventually lets their guard down. If my efforts where illegal, you might have called me an imbedded spy.

When I first moved into this town, I lived in an extended stay motel for a period while I attempted to find a place to live that both met my budget and which I found suitable and providing the amenities necessary to allow a longer stay.

My departure from Miami was in April 2008, and before I left, just within days before I left as I disposed of a great deal of furniture and personal items, I was nearing the closing on the sale of my home. I had already disposed of the mattress and box springs, all large furniture, and virtually everything else in my home that I didn't see as necessary or absolutely desirable to keep. My sleep would be on several comforters and a pile of pillows—but then so, it would also be the same place where I would recline to meditate.

Meditation is wonderful for clearing the head and seeking God's Word and especially to ask for the guidance for our daily lives. This night still in my Miramar town home, as I meditated and while home was pretty well emptied of all goods, I was surprised by the vision I received. The vision told me of soon-to-be-realized events and associations coming in my new home in my intended destination in Louisiana.

Meditation is really just self-hypnosis with a purpose. As I quieted myself and my breathing fell into the regular relaxing rhythm I seek, I began to experience a new bit of information from God. God let me know who I was soon to meet in my new home state. A series of faces came—one after another but unlike my experience of the viewing of my own lives, this was more of a gallery of people. One after another, mostly younger people in their 20's and early 30's it seemed, and finally ending with one person who I later came to know as Bobo.

Looking back, I did meet all of those people, mostly through associations as coworkers who worked at the Customer Service Call Center. Another point was made too: watch out for a snake. Do nothing to it, don't attempt to touch it as it will be highly poisonous. Just back off and leave it well enough alone.

I soon found work at the Customer Service Call Center and while still looking for a place to live, went to work. My experience certainly covered what the company was seeking, and seeing the large banner "We're Hiring" on the building give me quick access. The employment test was an automated system simulating a series of telephone calls and asking me details about the call, and giving some appropriate responses. We simply chose the best. In short order I was hired and began several weeks of training. I needed the job—not so much for the income though that was nice.

No, I needed the health insurance and my patience wore thin waiting for the 90 days qualification period to pass.

It was only another week or two before an apartment became available in the complex I had chosen, easily within walking distance of the new job. It all seemed well enough and I dealt with the inconvenience of having only limited household goods—no furniture, but enough cooking gear and folded blankets to set up a place to sleep. I carried with me a television and a stereo system—well selected in the first place and much easier to carry than to replace. I had a new home and I looked forward to new friends and new experiences.

What surprised me was that on a Friday night shortly after moving in, I stood in my bedroom tending to some minor chores when a very strange noise happened at the front door. My need for health insurance was to get a doctor's examination and medication for a problem that is fairly usual for a man getting on in years—an enlarged prostrate that causes some problem of what I would call a personal nature. Not a problem too large to bear, but one that required that I not be away from a rest room for more than an hour or two. There are commercials on television all the time for a prescription medication describing my exact problem. I had been living with that problem for about a year, and inconvenient as it was, it was tolerable since I had no prescription to deal with it and really had no alternative.

The sound at the front door was an invitation: a noisy sound that unmistakably said "Orgy!" while enveloped in a cascade of chimes or such. I was shocked and suddenly, being new in the complex, felt fearful, but I also said to myself that I just wasn't prepared to deal with this. I should have answered the door, but I couldn't muster the courage in the shocking confusion of the moment. I stood staring at the front door from the inside wondering if the sound would happen again, or if a knock would follow, but nothing further happened and I ignored the event and went back to my tasks.

The next Friday the event repeated itself—it was somewhere near eight o'clock in the evening and the same sound occurred. Again taking me by surprise as I had not realized the significance of the day nor of the time, and being still new in the area, I really thought this to be some kind of joke.

The problem was truly that I was new in the area and did not know anyone. What was happening, I wondered, and it came without warning or follow-up. I ignored this invitation too, reflecting on the week before and something that I had observed in the first few days of arriving in this little town.

I left Miramar, Florida on the 25th of April after the closing on the sale of my townhome, my second vehicle in tow on a rented auto transport trailer. My trip from Florida included a stop by to bid friends farewell in Vero Beach, and I spent several days leisurely driving the interstate from Florida to Alabama to Mississippi to Louisiana. With my cherished Celica on the auto trailer, and me behind the wheel of my Ford F-150, packed with all that it could carry, I limited my speed to a safe travel, and stopped only where I could easily maneuver the truck and carrier with my limited experience backing up with this trailer attached to my truck.

My father had been a Truck Rodeo National Champion, but a trailer behind me was an inconvenience, though a necessary one for these efforts. I was leaving my Florida life behind—I didn't want to do the same with my carefully tended, carefully used Celica, or any of the goods that I decided I could not live without which filled every nook and cranny of the truck, the truck bed which had a camper top and into every corner to those same cherished goods filled the interior of the Celica and its trunk too.

Finally in temporary residence at an extended stay hotel in Louisiana, I could drop that trailer and do a little exploring of the area. I love to just head out and see what is out there, and on one Friday night, I headed out to follow the directional markers indicating the next closest town.

There were no bright lights or places of excitement in the town I was in, so I hoped for the best and just followed my instincts. Driving several miles and thinking that I had to be getting to the next town, I was amazed by the lack of development. Few houses and no businesses interrupted my travel, a steel girder bridge crossed a small river and led me to a two-lane road dotted with a few far spaced street lights.

After driving a good distance and seeing no light illuminating the horizon, I did see a large, red barn on the right side of the road, and what looked like a school or perhaps an institution slightly up a hill. The barn could have been built anytime—it was iconic in shape, and as the sun's light faded as the day waned, it took on a hue that appeared rust colored. Indeed, it was rust colored as later drive-bys confirmed. It appeared abandoned, as each of the windows had been boarded from the inside with what is probably plywood. I ignored the barn and institutional building, and continued driving but seemed to make no progress in finding civilization. After a while, assuming that I was now heading out to more of rural Louisiana, I turned around and planned my return to my extended stay motel. I had travelled perhaps twenty minutes beyond the barn and now I was heading back in the opposite direction—it would take another twenty minutes just to get that far, of course.

As I approached that barn, now some time since I had first passed it, there was the most amazing of sights. For having passed almost no cars going in either direction, and seeing no real activity anywhere, I was amazed to see that there was a line of cars coming from the direction of the town where I now lived. That line of cars could have been a scene out of "Field of Dreams" in its length and appearance.

As far as I could see, a line of cars approached the barn where I now saw a guard house—now illuminated, and even a person standing in the middle of the street directing traffic. As I approached I slowed cautiously and out of curiosity too, and even though I did not have a turn signal on, the traffic guard stopped the line to allow me to turn into the barn. I had no reason to be directed there, and still with Florida plates on my truck, slowly drove straight on my original course heading back to my motel home.

As I drove, I passed vehicle after vehicle until I came to the end of the line, but saw in the distance more vehicles apparently coming from town to join the line into the barn too. The time was about 8:30 PM, and the sun had fully set as this was early May, and the days were far from the length they would be at the start of summer which was about a month and a half away.

I did not put the two events together immediately, unknowing that the line of cars and the invitation to "Orgy" were somehow related.

As I got to know Bobo better and continued to work at the Customer Service Call Center, events began to overlap. Bobo was at my home one Wednesday evening when he brought up the rust colored barn part in conversation, and part by error. He had a look on his face that said to me "I found out—I'm coming too" until he realized that the look on my face said that I was not party to this new found activity. Working at the Customer Service Call Center I had seen and discussed aspects of the Community Orgy—those who spoke to me didn't realize I was not a participant. Very logically they didn't know, I learned, in that there were actually five places in the general area used for this activity, though I knew the location of only one.

All it ever takes to infiltrate a community, if that is the right word used here for the knowledge of activity, is to agree, seem knowledgeable, and stay out of the direct discussion.

Listening is an activity beneficial in all aspects of life. Close listening—paying attention to detail—opens a wealth of information and knowledge whether you are supposed to have it or not. It comes from inadvertent comments like that made by a Director of the Service Center who lamented that he "was having a hard time convincing his daughters" to become participant in the "local tradition". He asked me for my advice before closing the discussion quickly with "oh, why am I asking you?" His wife did not escape the comments either, a manager at the same facility, who one of my co-workers said "had a definite interest in the young studs." Said to me assuming that I knew anyway, but not knowing that I had not joined the group.

Bobo realized his mistake too and I did not keep pressing. I had been in town a year before I met Bobo, working all that time in the Customer Service Call Center and seeing that there was some sort of ritual involved. You could not work in the place without seeing the undercurrents among many of those who worked there. As new employees were hired, strange things began to happen. The ritual started with cutting of hair—for the men, a buzz cut came, for the girls and women, the dying of a part of their hair. Know too that all of this was tied with an unusual interest in Mardi Gras.

The town even has a local holiday on Tuesday before Ash Wednesday, the traditional end of Mardi Gras and the beginning of Lent. The annual events, called Mardi Gras Balls, were held on Monday evening and went well into Tuesday. I recall a conversation just a few days before Mardi Gras between a clerk at a Tuxedo Rental store and a mother picking up two sets of formal wear for her children: "They won't be worn for long, but I want both of them to look good when presented," referring to her children. When I then was to be served by the same clerk, for my pick up of dry cleaning, I was asked which ball I was going to. Declining a suggestion that I was going to any, the clerk quickly mummed up.

It was amusing how her very words so quickly became lodged in her throat. I wasn't trying to be mean, I just did not have a quick reply to what was her innocent question about a very unusual ceremony.

When Bobo called the day after our awkward discussion regarding the old barn he cancelled a dinner that I was preparing at home. My deep and abiding love for him took a strange form in that I was looking at the same soul that had been my wife 2000 years ago, and at least too an incarnation in Atlantis some 30,000 years ago. As I said, it took the form of a fatherly association in this lifetime and he was a project and a duty asked by and accepted for God.

I acquiesced easily to Bobo's cancellation, not having any real leverage anyway. I simply prepared dinner and ate alone. Later that evening, I meditated and during that meditation I was given his real activity—he was doing drugs and was with a small group of men engaged in sex. If not that I fully capitulate to God's will at all times, I might have been angered at what I was being shown. The scene showed me at least two men who I did not know but later came forefront as part of the gay scene in this small town. If there is any activity that destroys the hope and joy of life, it is random sex and drug use. In this town there was both. Here that destruction surfaced little by little and the small town glimmer faded as more was revealed. It was also the start of a flow of information from God that revolved around the strange community activity and the small parties that I soon recognized were happening all around me.

This same event also caused my relationship with Bobo to take a new direction. Instead of being prominent in his week, he found ways to exclude me. Generally Monday through Thursday were for me, I bought food after all, but Friday and the weekend were almost never available any longer. The orgies were on Friday, and even though Bobo would confirm that he would be available for pickup for something I suggested, he would never be at his room at the cabinet shop. No, there was never an acknowledgement or an explanation, he had cut me out but God made sure I stayed in touch. I've said to many as I related this strange time in my life that had my promise been made to Bobo, I would have broken my promise easily and with real justification. No, my promise was made to God and that promise is not broken. Not now, not then, not ever. Suicide is breaking a promise to God, I had done that once in my series of incarnations, and breaking this promise with God to take care of Bobo was not going to be the result of my work.

God gives you nothing more than you can handle, but those limits are surely reached so often when running the gauntlet for your maker. Soon the pattern of Friday nights was established, and unless I had a better option—a trip perhaps, Friday was not on my schedule to be with Bobo as Bobo would scheme and lie then disappear often until Sunday night.

The orgies had a ritualistic association with them. From my workplace, I observed the kids—many who seemed to be recent high school graduates—who apparently were solicited and had their hair shaved quite short, and bits of dye in them. Almost as if dye had been held between two fingers and applied along a lock of hair. The women did not have their heads shaved as the men did, but did have the hair dye applied along locks too. My meditation served me well, bringing images of the evening's events and occasional discussions with God, who instructed me on steps to take, not to take, or asking me time after time if I was ready to stop helping Bobo, thus declining the completion of my promise. I continued to confirm my promise to help, knowing that my work was as much for me as it was for Bobo.

There was one time that as I meditated that God came showed me a strange set up that looked like stalls in the old barn—a group of people that were good "matches" for the subject, who in this case was Bobo. I was told that I was to bid for him, that my bid was to be high, and that my bid was to be high immediately, without benefit of run up as you would do in an auction. Those were firm instructions to me.

In meditation it is easy enough to see and hear, but there is an ethereal quality about it, like seeing the image but having it fuzzy about the edges. I was told the amount to bid, and given firm instruction for the process. Later in the week the unfolding of the event came during meditation and I remembered the discussion and the bid I was to make.

It was almost as if I had gone "all in" in a poker hand and had experienced the guffaws and the gasps of disbelief. I did as I was told, and the image faded. A couple weeks later, Bobo told me without being solicited that "he had selected me." I had won the auction—an auction that I neither saw, nor participated in, and because Bobo would not say anything beyond that simple comment, something I never had the right to question. Bobo did both crack cocaine and crystal methamphetamine at these orgies, and the associated anxiety and schizophrenic symptoms led him to outrageous acts, sometimes making me the subject of his anger. The town and area is a center of drug addiction and also for HIV infection and I hold no misconceptions as to why that is the case. Fuel irresponsible acts with irresponsible drugs and there can be no other outcome.

God gave me detail as time went on, telling me that Bobo had AIDS, and letting me plea to be his surrogate, my tears wailing as I explained that my life was nearing the end and asking God to let me carry the burden. My thoughts were that Bobo might at some point re-establish a relationship with his daughter who when he spoke of her, always seemed to express love. It was the only time I ever heard him speak of his emotions. Every other feeling I expected of Bobo seemed to be locked somewhere, never the world to see. Except for anger of course, which the drugs would occasionally cause to erupt without warning.

My association with Bobo did bring some strange psychic experiences too. Once he mentioned that he had engaged in a sexual act while at the same time doing crack cocaine at 4 AM. The image of that event, the other participant in a compromising position, and even the act of inhalation of the drug suddenly came into my mind. From Bobo's memory to my active mind, I knew and saw the act. Too, Bobo would sometimes leap from his seat and dance, and I would stand in amazement wondering what he was doing. On one occasion though, I did not have to ask. When Bobo was swaying to the unseen band, I actually heard the music that was playing in his head. I have to admit, the music was very good. It was playing in my head too, if only for a moment.

My discovery of Bobo was on May first, 2009, and the turmoil began quite quickly, and the association was intense and difficult, but moderated and advised by God. The whole room would seem filled with the Word of God when He spoke, and I would cry out for help and the calm resolve would be returned to me so I was able to get through all of this. As we approached October 2009 though, Bobo would advise me that changes were on the way—his prophetic ability still intact despite the drugs and aberrant behavior—and he warned me that he had to leave soon.

I didn't know what to do, and I kept my opinion to myself considering the outbursts that occasionally resulted when I tried to discuss anything.

One morning at about 1 AM my sleep was interrupted by a cell phone call (my work at the Customer Service Call Center allowed me a very generous call plan that I passed to Bobo preferring to keep my long established plan) from Bobo who had decided that he could no longer work or live in Louisiana. He wanted to go to California as soon as he could. He gave no explanation but gave me an ultimatum: go with him (actually I would take him) or not see him again.

By this time, my patience with Louisiana had long since been exhausted anyway. Most small towns have charming people, interesting local traditions, and hope. Shackled with this strange local custom of orgies and sex parties, I'm sure an undercurrent of shame for the participants, and surely with the difficulty and connections for drugs that Bobo had in the town, I was ready to leave.

It took nearly a couple of weeks to make it happen though—my cherished Celica had to be sold, some goods either sold or donated and my worldly goods reduced to that which would fit into my full size pickup truck. The expense and distance of going to California precluded taking my Celica and a buyer from nearby was thrilled to find my sale listing on the local Craig's List.

I still relied on the knowledge that God, who speaks when He chooses to speak, would be there. Bobo lived with me for the next week still tied to the tumultuous friends he had made, and the addictions he pursued. God's help was there, as I did quickly sell my Celica and managed to sell most of the furniture I had.

If it couldn't be packed into small boxes to be packed into the truck, or if it was too valuable to dispose of at a fair price, then my last minute option was a storage unit. I rented a storage unit on the main thoroughfare that heads out of town as I quickly learned that Bobo was more interested in maintaining his ties to his drug friends than to participate in the work of moving.

My orderly approach as a career man in logistics was a bit helter skelter, but I persevered in the process of packing to leave anyway.

We finally left knowing that lack of sufficient notice to the apartment complex meant that my security deposit would be forfeited-an understandable but undesirable expense. I left a few things in the apartment knowing that I could not take them, that they were not valuable enough to put into the storage unit, but there was no severe damage to the apartment unit and it was cleaned well too.

I have again a small Sheltie, a darling I named Sara, and fleas in Louisiana are on a rampage—I was always taking steps for her comfort but I made sure even to set a flea bomb before we locked the door at 7 PM, after dark in mid October, dropping the keys into the slot at the apartment complex office as we rolled out of the complex heading for California.

The trip was largely uneventful but it seemed ominous that just as I was driving out of the complex the truck's "check engine" light came on—I've never had to deal with this before, a fact that Bobo scoffed at as if that possibility didn't exist. This potential mechanical condition caused me concern though. Besides the weight of the full truck load, there was a person I hoped would be coming down from whatever drugs still existed in his body, my dog on my lap, but my concern held knowing that Bobo was a bit erratic.

I wanted to conserve money on the trip—it was always my concern as Bobo took no interest in our welfare as long as his demands were met. I shared that we would make a stop at a motel every other night to allow a better night sleep, and the ability to shower and shave—an act to rejoin the human race with a clean shaven face and clean clothes. We were traveling with money constraints so I didn't count on Bobo's demand for beer as we drove—his drugs and anxiety did fuel a simple inability to ride along peacefully. It was already late when we left and picking up the interstate only took a few minutes. There were two or three exits for the interstate in town, and I saw them as escape routes.

We left the State of Louisiana on Interstate 20 a couple of hours later, entering Texas. That was my initial goal and I focused on looking for a rest area.

I tried to avoid the subject and even tried to have Bobo understand why I didn't want to spend money but a nearly outraged Bobo made me stop for beer, again exhibiting agitation and threatening me if I did not stop. I spied an exit with a convenience store and a gas pump. It was not yet midnight, so pulling off I got gas and Bobo went for beer with my money. Damned if you do, and damned if you don't. I knew that I was spending money for a bad time, but having a person try to attack you while driving is counterproductive too.

Quickly reentering the interstate, I pulled into the first rest area we encountered. Bobo consumed that beer before sleeping. Wishing only that I had so peaceful a slumber, I found it necessary to keep one eye on Bobo. My rest was fitful as rain caused the truck windows to fog and then there was the noise and lights of the constant arrival and departure of cars and trucks, and the droning highway sound of vehicles on the interstate just a few feet from the rest area.

We only had the bench seat on which to sleep, and sleeping sitting up in a small area doesn't allow the body to rest. It never left my mind that I was doing the work God had asked me to do, but it was not a pleasant task. Secretly and quietly, I prayed to God until I managed to get two hours of sleep that night.

The sun was somewhere over the horizon and I started the truck again, after stretching to see what was in the rest area vending machines. Bobo did the same, no longer pressing me for alcohol. Doing the best we could to look anything but disheveled, I got a couple of hours driving under way before stopping for breakfast. Bobo seemed comfortable riding along. At least as I drove during the day he would nap, and even played with the dog from time to time. After that first night on the road, he no longer demanded beer and I assumed it was because he was also not using drugs.

Loving someone is difficult when they are self-abusing, as is the case with drug users. The kindness and concern you know you have for someone is difficult to apply when the results of your efforts are simply rejected or when they are violently opposed.

The rest of the trip was uneventful—the fields of wind turbines in Western Texas, the airplane graveyard we passed, and the sheer beauty of the landscape we saw as the interstate weaved between boulders that took on beautiful shapes and colors from the ever changing light and landscape. Entering California was a relief indicating that the journey for now at least was nearing an end. The interstate itself showed signs of wear which I thought odd. Pot holes dotted the shoulder of the interstate causing me to be extra careful knowing that a slight move out of the traffic lane could result in damage to the truck, and surely its contents.

Chapter Ten

We stopped at a motel for the night to recoup and refresh and found a takeout Mexican restaurant. I did not dare mention alcohol in any form, not wanting to entice Bobo to ask or demand more. He seemed less anxious, and now being several days away from his drugs he seemed more settled. A walk in the night air was refreshing.

As we gassed up the next morning, I asked the attendant about the road ahead and was surprised to learn that the interstate would expand in the number of lanes and that maintenance was much better. We also learned that we were only a couple of hours from Los Angeles, our intended destination.

We had breakfast from the motel buffet and set out again to complete the trip, this bringing us to enter Los Angeles as a rude layer of filth hovered over the city ahead of us. The smog was heavy, and this was mid October. A long severe grade in the interstate made me wonder if my brakes were sufficient with the full load in the bed of the truck. Having a camper top on the truck bed gave us the ability to carry more goods, but it added weight and I tried to be cautious as gravity exerted its efforts to take the truck well above the posted speed limit. Others may drive this highway daily and are used to the changes, but I was a novice. The hills in South Florida are in Hialeah, they say, but I had never seen them even though I lived in the area for eighteen years. It was a joke, of course, since you could practically see to Tampa since Florida is just so flat.

When I drove cross country in 1974, I recall the extreme drop on Interstate 80 into the Salt Lake City area, but my car then was small and maneuverable. I still kept close eyes on the runaway truck areas prepared should I feel necessary to use it. Here, coming into Los

Angeles, the only thing on the side of the interstate was litter, and beyond the barrier fences were houses.

We were both surprised how quickly the interstate brought us into downtown Los Angeles, and with all my worldly goods just a few inches behind my head, I had no plans to stop in the city. We continued on the road, and found myself somehow heading out of the city to areas north. I wanted a little more of wide open spaces, or at least a good place to park. We had arrived but knew not where and a search for home had just begun.

Checking for apartments lasted a couple of days before accepting the fact that a decent rental was going to cost considerably more than a comparable rental in Louisiana.

Having been confronted with this reality, I chose to seek a location outside of the Los Angeles area, a place I had visited on business a few years prior, Palmdale.

Out past Santa Clarita on the way to Lancaster and Edwards Air Force Base was Palmdale—a "close the windows and lock the doors at 5 PM 'cause you're in for the night" kind of place. I ended up living there for a year and a half to April 2011but Bobo was there for only about a month and a half.

The whole experience there with Bobo was exasperating—somehow he managed a drug connection almost immediately. He said the voices from the other side directed him, and I believe it. Just because you die does not make you better—as people of principle, you always need to judge your own actions against your concept of God. I use a good way to separate the wheat from the chafe: I ask simply "Is this God's will?" Using that simple determinate has helped me keep the evil thoughts away, and to steadfastly rely on the good advice I receive.

Bobo never seemed to apply that logic or any good logic for that matter. Bobo did whatever his voices asked and did so by justifying the requests from his voices on the other side by saying they wanted him drunk, or high, or engaged in some activity so they could experience his experiences vicariously. I consider it wisdom to reach just as high as possible for guidance—sincerely ask God, and God will reply.

Bobo's voices led him to leave the motel on the first night in Palmdale and he quickly found drugs, and the chaos began again.

Listening to music videos on the laptop computer had Bobo banging on the desktop, screaming as he sang in strange duet with music videos, but as the hour grew late Bobo would eventually relent to going to sleep as our search for an apartment began anew each day. I always said a prayer of thanks when he climbed into bed to sleep—he would sleep through the night.

After two days in Palmdale I secured a six month lease for a two bedroom apartment—not the most upscale of places—but with payment of six months' rent in advance I was able to get the lease in place. A drug and alcohol addicted person is hazardous to your sanity, welfare, assets and all that you hold dear. Off on a chaotic night just a day or two into the lease, Bobo tries to attack me and the police were called by a neighbor, thankfully. He was transported to a rehabilitation facility where he remained for several days before I was called to pick him up. I did go pick him up and I was optimistic that things just might be better. My hopes were dashed almost immediately as stopping for lunch just minutes later, he immediately found alcohol and I chose to leave him in Echo Park, an area of Los Angeles where the facility was located.

Several days later, life on the street had taken its toll and I went back the area and retrieved Bobo again. This visit to my apartment—more a visit than sharing a residence—lasted again for only a couple of days and the process was repeated. The police were called, this time by me, and off to a rehabilitation facility again. A couple of weeks passed this time as he had been treated and then shuffled to a drug-free half way house with a heavy religious orientation. I picked him up, this was Saturday, December 4th, and he seemed more relaxed. The evening went well and there was no alcohol or drugs involved, but he did want new shoes so we found some the next day at a store in Palmdale's mall. Sunday started with breakfast which he proudly prepared in the fashion that his step-father, Manuel, had done often it seemed.

That evening, now December 5th at 8:30 PM, I was surprised to see Bobo march out of his bedroom with a daypack strapped to his back and head straight for the apartment door. I realized quickly what was happening and grabbed my keys and coat and tried to follow. Bobo was a distance ahead of me now and was leaving the gate of the apartment complex as I tried to catch up.

Following him, I turned once to the end of the block and started to turn again to follow him into the night darkness. He faded as I shouted for him to stop, but he was gone. I stood there for a while trying to take in what was happening.

Bobo had left without explanation or goodbye. I went home and took inventory of what was in his room. He carried only a few things and I suddenly realized why he had me buy him thermal long-johns earlier as we looked for shoes.

His old shoes sat there, and more things that he had acquired from me over our period together but it was obvious that he had gone. He had planned the departure all weekend but discussed none of it.

Resigned to these events, I lay in bed that night thinking of the loss of Bobo. It was God's request that I take care of him, my love for him returned by God's grace on the first night I met him back in Louisiana. I knew from dream that Bobo was the same soul that was my wife in 30,000 BC in Atlantis and that incarnation a big part of my karma for this lifetime. Bobo described our time together in Rome some 2,000 years ago. The drugs and alcohol destroying his life today prevented him from completing some karmic needs—I was apparently the key to his overcoming those issues in this lifetime.

It was perhaps ten days later that my guides gave me a short, terse message about Bobo that said simply that he was in a hospital. With the message were some images that confirmed that it was again a rehabilitation facility, but I did not know where. Bobo apparently had found drugs again and went on a rampage, a rampage that affected only him but landed him in police custody again.

Just a couple days later I got a call from somewhere, the caller would not identify himself well enough for me to glean information, confirming that my cell number was a valid contact number for Bobo. I confirmed that it was, but told them that he was not with me right now. They knew that, but still told me nothing. I assumed that the call was from the rehabilitation center but that they had no permission to release information.

A couple of months later I called that number again hoping that Bobo was in the facility getting help. He had left some time before, but he had not contacted me for return. My feelings were mixed. Doing as God asked had carried me through this difficult time, knowing that the soul of Bobo was at least twice my wife in prior incarnations and a difficult friend this lifetime. I prayed to God and meditated as well as I could, but the separation was still difficult.

It was perhaps two weeks later that standing in the kitchen I suddenly felt the presence of God, and He began to speak. We had a conversation about Bobo, starting just where my concerns had left off. Had he, referring to Bobo, returned to me, he (Bobo) would have returned with a sense of entitlement. Bobo would have come back feeling that whatever was mine would have been his too. I had already lost enough by Bobo damaging items, a computer and portable printer had walked off as exchange for cash for drugs.

Access to my bank account and even pocket cash had always been secured from prying eyes and sticky fingers, but Bobo's return would have left me destitute. After taking advantage of what he could, Bobo would have moved on. God's explanation did not relieve the pain I endured but I would get over that. God's explanation did let the feeling of failure pass, knowing for sure now that the job I promised to do for Bobo at God's request thirty years prior had been concluded,

I wrote to Bobo's family in Dallas asking for them to let me know if he returned and I heard nothing for several months. It was on June 25 that I got a text message from his sister-in-law. The text was short—Bobo had committed suicide that day in Fort Worth, Texas. He had hanged himself near a homeless shelter. Almost in total disbelieve, I called the Fort Worth Police Department who confirmed the disturbing news.

Bobo's sister-in-law said that I was the only person who Bobo seemed to care about, that I was the only person who took an interest in him. Apparently Bobo took an interest in me too. Difficult as it was, Bobo was thanking me for all that I had done for him.

Over the course of our relationship, I had taken a number of photographs of Bobo—random shots generally without his knowledge. He always seemed content with me taking them but he would never allow me to have him pose, and he didn't concern himself with appearances either. After he left my home in December, I thought that I would do something to help me move on. I chose to prepare a disk of all the photos and send them to his family. There was no reply, no thank you from anyone, just silence to any phone message I left. The text was enough, and I did speak to the sister-in-law about funeral details telling her at first that I could not attend. My funds were low but I found a way that I could rent a high gas-mileage vehicle and make the trip by driving. I was able to see Bobo's family and home.

I got to Dallas in good order and stayed again at a La Quinta Inn, and went to the funeral home the next day, my first contact with any relative of Bobo's. They were what I would call a strange lot. Bobo's older brother was dealing with drug addiction too but making steps to stay clean. The mother is largely non-communicative, at least with me, and the family home a perfect example of poverty in a poverty ridden neighborhood. Everyone in the area seemed to be eking out a life as best they could. Small homes that were old, outdated, and in need of repair line the street and the surrounding area. Living day to day and perhaps hour to hour was the lot of these people, an environment on the surface that can only hope is at least loving, for material items were in very short supply.

My first face-to-face meeting with any relative came at the service. Bobo had been cremated so there was no viewing, or at least not one where I had been invited to attend. There was an opportunity and I took the time even before leaving Palmdale to prepare remarks.

I spoke as did one other person at Bobo's service—his ashes displayed in the urn that the family would keep. I told the story of how God asked me to take care of Bobo thirty years prior but hoping not to scare the mourners away, and doing my best to be honest too. I spoke of Bobo's adventurous side but added how drugs had destroyed his young life.

I met Bobo's daughter, she was only ten years of age, and gave her the shoes Bobo had left behind in my home six months prior. I wanted her to have something of her father's and there was just not much to give. Shoes seemed to be the measure of the stature of the man. His daughter could look at the shoes to remember her father, hoping that the memory of a crack pipe would not be the first thought.

As soon as I finished speaking, the minister who conducted the service rushed to the podium and announced to the mourners that "none could come to the father except through Christ." I didn't bother to contradict him. The truth is the truth, and religion isn't truth. As we all pass from this life, we all will know the truth.

When I entered Bobo's family home following the service, I was amazed to see that the pictures I had taken of Bobo and eventually sent to the family on disc had been enlarged, printed, framed, and multiple copies produced. The mother who would barely share a word with me quietly gave those photos to cousins, friends, and others though I did not know the relationship of those people. I was not acknowledged and I was not offended by that fact either. Somehow I had played a part of documenting Bobo's life in a time and place where he would have been forgotten if not for my casual act. His family could see his face as it neared the end of his lifetime. His daughter could look upon the eyes and see the resemblance and point to her own children one day and say "this was your grandfather. This was my father."

I do not know God's full intent in having me take care of Bobo but I know that prior to Bobo's birth, Bobo chose me to take on the task for him and I accepted. Maybe it was payback or karma, but surely it was the love of one soul over eons for another soul. I am grateful for the opportunity to help and would gladly take on the pain and suffering to help another again. God loves all his children, and I know that these opportunities were an expression of God's love for me.

Chapter Eleven

God will always work in your life if you let him—in relationships, in the challenges you face each day, in the successes and in the failures. We learn by getting to the top and we learn by tumbling to the bottom. We beseech, we beg, we try to understand what God has in store for us but there is too that simple reality that that everything we encounter has for good or for evil been something that we have seen and agreed to for this life. Our problems and our challenges have all been presented to us before becoming incarnate.

When my guides told me as a first grader to go tell my teacher that I was George Mallory, which I promptly did, and my teacher firmly told me "No, you are not!" I was crushed and hurt. My guides and I had a discussion standing in a cow pasture not too far from my home that evening. I had crossed that cow pasture many, many times walking from my home to the school bus stop atop a nearby hill where the road allowed a reasonable route and room for the students to stand at a neighborhood candy store.

My discussion with my guides was simple—I asked if I had to do as they say, referring again to the instruction to tell my first grade teacher who I was. I recall at the time that I had my present day surname written on tablet paper in my halting first grade penmanship just so I would not forget the name. After all I was young, only six years of age, and we all start out in similar ways with the alphabet around the room in both capital and lower case letters, and basic colors identified with simple names in lettering that is easily read by children.

As I discussed the day with my guides, they responded "no" it was not necessary that I do as they asked, and in a most adult manner I said I realized that each lifetime is an opportunity to advance spiritually, and

I asked if I would achieve more if I went through this life without their help.

My guides told me that I would advance more quickly without their help. I recall stating that I knew the real challenges of my life would come late—at the age of 64 years in fact, though truthfully the years prior to age 64 have been no cake walk either. I asked my guides to return to me when I was 64 but fearing that real hope and real help might be excluded, I asked that God come through whenever He chose to do so. My guides agreed and I never questioned God.

I asked for that certain time, my age of 64, for the return assistance of my guides, but recall the feeling, the impression, of when their return would occur was different than the time I asked for. What I felt would be the time of their return is still pending. With profound relief I can say God has not failed to come through and has come through on many occasions.

The point here is that being alive is the opportunity to advance spiritually. We can apply many rationales, we can espouse many justifications, but we need always to remember that getting ahead by using the laws of God is why you are here. How that expression of spiritual advancement is achieved comes in many forms and is different for each and every person, just as each person has their own and specific karmic balance to achieve. The laws are the same for each person for they are God's laws, and you are the one to comply. Make it a good and sincere effort and progress and success are achieved.

Chapter Twelve

Most of us fear death—it is the unknown and even though we are all doomed to death, it is not easily accepted. Death rips us from those we love the most and leaves us with emptiness where warmth and hope resided. Death is not what we fear though for death is simply the return home to the place from which we came.

My abilities have afforded me a strange foresight for some at times. I do not choose with whom I can share the knowledge, but I clearly know that I share it as God would have me do. I have seen death forthcoming some persons in as little as 12 hours, and as long as nearly five years. At times I am well acquainted with the soon to be deceased, and at others times barely acquinted.

Unless you bring about your own death with intent, remember that death is merely the transition and the timing is right regardless of what you might consider as right. Death does pluck you out—with or without your anticipation or your agreement. Fear of the change or fear of the pain of death are unwarranted. Let me share some of the stories.

These stories will be without the ability to provide verification, but they were important for the recipient. Knowledge of our forthcoming demise allows a person to prepare for that demise—it need not be a statement of goodbye, or arranging for the smooth transfer of financial assets, but it does pervade the daily affairs of a person.

Anger is not pursued and vendettas become meaningless when our own eternity looms. An extra hug or a prolonged kiss is the more normal as we understand that there will be a separation soon. The living body will be left behind and the eternal soul returned to the realm of creation—that is the nature of death. It is easy, it is normal, and silently I've often said of those passing over "Hip, Hip, Hooray, You Made It!" in an acknowledgement of the end of a lifetime.

If we were to pray for the departed soul, pray that they were able to complete all the tasks while incarnate that they had agreed to in their Contract With God, their contract executed before a return to earth for the lifetime they were now leaving.

The earliest memory that I have where I predicted the impending death of someone occurred sometime in the mid 1970's at an after-hours discotheque in Center City Philadelphia called the DCA. This club was hot then, the premier destination for the regular clubs patrons who emptied the regular clubs and bars in Center City Philadelphia at the required 2 AM, filling the DCA with patrons who lived for the late night, or just wanting to continue the experience of the disco night. There was a line outside to get in at the DCA, a line at the counter of an adjoining open-this-late hoagie and cheese steak shop, and of course the one or two people who peddled their illicit wares. At that time the favorite illicit drugs were marijuana and poppers, the prescription drug amyl nitrate, a dance club favorite, in valid use it was for someone having a heart attack.

The DCA was within walking distance of most of the clubs and patrons of all kinds lined up. The DCA was the club that drew the crowd from the disco bars, the leather bars, the country and western bars and the dyke bars, all converging exactly at this hour for a three hour extension on the party night.

Most often either before we got there or shortly after everyone had by then too much to drink. For sheer spectacle, the dance floor was grand, the ceiling high and looking like a rotunda, loud, and slightly elevated as it sat under a canopy of lights and the disc jockey booth which loomed over us all, spitting out the best of the latest music for our nightly rituals. It was one of these nights.

As I moved around the perimeter of the dance floor, I came across someone that I had seen and perhaps spoken to only once. A young man, perhaps 22 but certainly not more years, tall and blond—a handsome young man in a gay bar. I glanced quickly at him but thought nothing of it until I found myself being forced in his direction by an unknown hand. Gushing the message, he looked at me strangely as I said "Oh my God, you're are going to die in about two years by decapitation." I was embarrassed at the proclamation, I was still young enough myself to be unsure of my own psychic bent. His name was George Montgomery, and I knew that he lived in North East Philadelphia. He said something but with the blaring music I could only see his mouth move—the words eluded me.

I somehow retain some of these thoughts that come through, while others come and go without my conscious retention, and those seem to leave persons in tears and me fully in an awkward predicament. For George, this was prophesy.

I hope that the warning was well served. I never see these things as having an option to change, rather they serve to prepare. It was about two years later that a small report of an automobile accident in the Philadelphia Inquirer caught my eye. Indeed, a George Montgomery of North East Philadelphia had been the passenger in an automobile that struck a utility pole, ejecting the passenger. That passenger was George, and he had been propelled from the car striking the guy wire for the pole, severing his head. There was not a great deal more information in the short report, but I was sure it was the person who had received the warning that night in Center City Philadelphia.

It was just a few days before Christmas in Miami when my department from my Cruise Line invited us all to a Christmas gambling night onboard a small gambling charter yacht. These events often bring people together who we know and work with, others we speak with but have never had the chance to meet due to far flung office locations and the like. Family members usually make up part of the group, and the introductions and small talk pervade the room as we wait for food service to start, just discussing the concerns of the day. These events are enjoyable and they offer us a chance to relax with the people we work with when so often the days demands keep us moving and focused on our tasks as hand. This was that same kind of night, and chatter and mingling was the order of the moment.

Up walked someone that I had never seen before, and even with the best of introductions a name will slip my mind from time to time. That person asked me unexpectedly "I understand that you're psychic. Is that true?" I replied that yes, I was psychic and I got the question that is really not too rare "when will I die?" he said. I was more surprised than taken aback and in I reply I said "I'm sorry, but nothing is coming through." I apologized and explained that such a reply was not unusual, and I've always thought that an empty reply simply meant that there was no compelling issue to contend with. This person seemed to understand and I was relieved.

"What about me?" said Raymond Gale, a thin, wirery man who we all looked at as the class clown. Raymond was an African-American, but reveled in getting a department meeting chuckling, or handling an important call in the least serious manner possible. He was a person of genuine warmth and care and professional in his work. Everybody knew and liked Raymond, he was just that kind of person. My reply was immediate and sad. I said "Oh Ray, I wish you hadn't asked. You will pass in not more than two to three months and it will be your heart." I didn't have the means to stop the reply and several people standing nearby heard the reply too. Raymond looked me straight in the eye but said nothing. He waited a few minutes then seemed to brush it off, and the evening continued without further dismal news.

The truth came just six weeks later.

Arriving at work one morning an email was on my computer and on all the computers at work. Raymond Gale had died of an apparent heart attack over the weekend. His car had been found at the side of the road and he was dead at the wheel. Raymond had succeeded in protecting others by pulling over even as he neared his own death. The prophesy given on board the gambling yacht had fulfilled and we all had lost a friend.

The wake was not a place to ask, but as members of the department chatted with the grieving family, I could not help wonder if he had taken the information seriously and gotten his affairs in order. Indeed, if he were able to say goodbye to his wife and family.

The Miami Herald article had the picture of Charley Riggs right there on the first page of the Local section on September 25, 1995. I was surprised to see it and read under the headline "Mom visits death scene hoping to find answers." The prophesy for Charley had come full circle from proclamation to finality. "Right after her son was murdered . . ." it went on and I read with sadness and resignation that again a life had ended as had been told by me to the departed soul. This was a follow up story, the death had occurred on September 21, 1994 in South Dade.

Charley was to my knowledge a nice fellow, not that much younger than I was, and someone who kind of stumbled into my life for a brief period when I lived along Biscayne Boulevard in Miami in the 6200 block. It was a nice gated apartment complex, and was sometime between December 1991 and December 1992, when I moved from there to another building some 36 blocks south and almost in another world with the change of neighborhood. Though my complex was somewhat secure, just in the few blocks north of us was the area of prostitutes and pimps, cheap motels, and with all of that, drugs. I am rather naïve about much of this scene, giving up alcohol and living a nicely normal life since 1984 though confronted with all of the trials and turmoil that society heaps on each of us today, seemingly to test our will and our mettle.

I had been working with the Cruise Line for a while and the income was steady and I was optimistic about the future.

My move from East Tennessee to Miami was finally feeling comfortable and I was even acclimating to the heat and humidity of South Florida. This climate is sub-tropical and the climate does take a bit of time to get used to but I eventually would change clothing style and fabric weight and the feeling was good. I felt good about myself and I was more open to meeting others. Charley was just someone I met at a convenience store and we struck up a conversation one day. I did not realize that he was in the throes of his addiction—he just seemed a nice fellow.

We talked then about anything and it was not for but a few minutes—keeping it light, if you will. The introduction occurred then followed by a short, funny chat. From there it was on with our lives. Charley was quite affable, I thought.

Since I was new in the neighborhood in North East Miami, I welcomed this new friend. Coincidentally I had moved from the same general area where Charley would die in South Dade.

Times were tough for me, I did not have a car then, my 1988 Toyota Corolla had been repossessed for missing just one payment and I scrambled to get my affairs in order, but being both late and no longer in Tennessee, I somehow triggered the repo man. The action had me walking in the neighborhood more often than I wanted. I ran into Charley a couple times and he always said hello.

Having no friends in the area and Charley seeming to be a good candidate for one, I invited him back to my home for coffee one day. We sat and talked, generally making jokes which he seemed so prone to do, and with me playing the fall guy, the laughter went on. His revelation that he was related to Bobby Riggs, the tennis pro who took on Billy Jean King in the televised "Battle of the Sexes" which Riggs lost surprised and interested me. Charley was the great-nephew but he chose not to go too much about that—he didn't know much more than that it seems, or didn't find it enough of interest to discuss the facts at length of the match.

What a small world, I chuckled to myself.

As Charley got up to leave and I was leading him to the door, I got a sudden psychic insight and immediately shared it with him: he was going to die in a little more than two years and it would be by gunshot.

Charley was a Sagittarius, he had told me, usually light hearted and playful, but this news brought him to a serious frame of mind immediately and he looked me in the eye. I explained that such predictions were not uncommon for me to make, and sadly I also explained that the outcome was usually accurate. I suggested he get his affairs in order, and to avoid circumstances that might lead to the predicted end. That was the last time I saw Charley as my life and work continued, and I moved down Biscayne Boulevard only 37 blocks, but to a new neighborhood and a new view of Biscayne Bay.

Charley's life took its course too leading him to that morning in South Dade that was punctuated with a gunshot.

The article in the Miami Herald brought full circle the prediction about Charley's death. With the information in the article as my guide, I tried to locate his mother but was unsuccessful in doing so. Shirley Riggs should know that her son was aware of his pending demise, that his life had reached the expected end whether or not he had prepared well for it. The news story told me that Charley was doing drugs and that was something that I did not know—I said I was naïve and my short association never tipped me to the fact but from where and how I met Charley, in hindsight, I should have known. I always see the best in people until proven wrong—sometimes an expensive and perplexing fact.

This was no lesson, just the nagging thought that a truly warm person had lost a life to a single bullet propelled more by drug use than gunpowder.

Before I had moved to the apartment on Biscayne Boulevard at the Banyon Bay Apartments, ironically I had lived in the very area where Charley was to lose his life.

I knew the bar he had last been seen in but only from passing it on my way north—I had never seen the inside of the building nor set foot on the property. My world was different there—I stayed briefly with an Aunt who was kind, meticulous, and so resembled my mother. They were two sisters who were always close, and who married first cousins too.

Charley was tangled in the weird world of drugs and it strangled the life out of him. A kind, loving soul whose time on earth drew to a close too quickly to have accomplished all that could have been. He'll have another opportunity, as we all do, to move from aspiration to that level where we join again with God. In the period between lives, we have opportunity to learn and reflect on each life—the most recent life and all the lives and issues that have gone before to prepare for the next incarnation. We look for advancement, we seek success with the goal of rejoining God always our goal. I wish the best for Charley and hope that he is doing all he can now if discarnate to achieve that.

If incarnate, I pray he makes better choices in life. Asking for God's help is always wise. Even wiser is to accept God's help.

My neighbor Shirley Carter stood in the kitchen of my father's modest home in Tennessee as my father sat at the kitchen table smoking a cigarette. It was a general conversation, more to pass the day than to address any of the world's pressing issues. My father seemed unconcerned about taking good care of himself, but Shirley was a terrific neighbor, and frankly a long term tenant too.

My father lived in the modest home but rented out a large two-apartment building immediately adjacent that he had near single-handedly built at a younger age. Shirley often stepped in to check on him, the kind of sympathetic kindness that the south is known for.

I lived elsewhere, though close, and I was considering moving soon. Being in East Tennessee, even being born here, didn't make the grade when thoughts of a vibrant lifestyle crept in. My boyhood home outside of Philadelphia offered all that was possible for an area rich in cultural development, historical significance, and trendy restaurants, and the abundance of news outlets and a world class highway system. It was true, having seen the lights of the city I just wasn't content with living in the slow paced, small town community where I then felt that I was being suffocated. I considered moving again to Florida, this time it would be Miami which offered a year-round economy and a climate said to be "ten degrees cooler in summer, and ten degrees warmer in winter" than the west coast of Florida.

Since visiting Miami at age 10 on a trip for a National Truck Rodeo with my father as a contender for a national title, I had always wanted to live in the sub-tropical climate. Like any other conversation, it was just a lazy way to pass the time on a warm spring day.

My father started the conversation with something that said he was getting old, that it was time to go home. I contradicted him, saying without thought that there would be four and a half years yet. Shirley laughed, and repeated the prophesy to my father, calling him in her southern drawl "Well, Ray, what do you think of that. Can you hang on for another four and half years? Gene says you're going to have to!" Though I now use the same name as my father, Ray, it wasn't until I went to Miami in very early 1990 that everyone called me Gene to differentiate me from Ray, my father. Ray replied "I'll guess I'll have to" but didn't say much more than that. It wasn't a conversation topic, the my prophesy just kind of slipped out, as that kind of thing does with me. There are times when I feel that words almost belch out—me unable to control their coming, and it could be in a few short words or on occasion a full-fledged reading.

I have run into people on the street, known and unknown, who receive a full reading on the spot, an example of which I'll relate shortly as it has come true for a person who has entered the national limelight. I always say that I'm letting God speak through me, truth is I cannot stop it anyway, and I suffer the awkwardness or embarrassment that accompanies that act. Oh well, if that is all the weight I have to carry to do God's work, I'm glad I can be of service and that really is a small price to pay.

My father was an obstinate man—I've seen him stomp his feet when he didn't get his way and growing up there was the problem where he would promote an argument with a family member—either my mother or me but never my brother—as a means of letting him storm out of the house.

I realize now that the maneuver was his means to get out of the house to go to a bar to drink, but then it was upsetting. My family didn't address alcohol as a problem. That was unfortunate but growth is the key and other groups now offer a comforting approach to problems to be dealt with but not created by those who must deal with them.

There was no explanation to the prophesy, just the statement of time and as life went on, no milestones marked. It wasn't until Shirley reminded me of the prophesy after my father passed that we realized that the timing was on mark. The four and a half years had encompassed two bouts with pneumonia, our attempt to have Ray take better care of himself by securing an assisted living situation in Chattanooga near my brother, that allowed my father to come and go pretty much as he wished, and to visit my brother whenever he cared to do so. Problem was, once my father had returned to health following the first pneumonia, he promptly declared himself fit and moved back into the very situation we had worked so hard to change. As you might expect, failing to take care of himself became a recurrent theme, and after time he again contracted pneumonia, this time ending up in the Veteran's Administration Hospital in the next town over. This visit did not result in his recovery, and his passing occurred as was predicted.

How exactly close to the prediction of my father's death the event came, I don't recall enough of the detail. The initial statement was just an afternoon conversation, general in nature, but since it occurred just before I left the area for Miami, and the death occurring in September 2004, the four and a half years was there. Some predictions are more general, but I have had some that are just pinpoint accurate, as the next event I'll describe before moving onto other events in this psychic life.

Chapter Thirteen

When I left Louisiana with Bobo for California, the situation was very stressful. It was abrupt, and I was dealing with a person whose major concern was to try to find drugs. I wanted out of Louisiana quickly, but I just could not see tossing caution to the wind. I sold a car and some furniture quickly, gave much to charity, but could not part with other items that were both expensive and high quality. Not everything I wanted to take would fit into the bed of my pickup truck even though I had a secure camper top. Bobo was not helping much, so I relieved some issues by securing a storage unit. After Bobo left me in California, I contemplated what to do and decided just to wait, hoping for his return. When God finally returned to explain that Bobo's return to me would be contrary to my best interest, I decided that having goods in two places was too scattered, and I needed to consolidate my affairs. I planned a return to Louisiana.

The trip back to Louisiana in February 2010 was a reprieve from the boredom of Palmdale, California and I relished in using a new GPS device. For once I could set a destination and my map was suddenly laid out for use. The best part of it all was that I could plan my stops to maximize travel without necessarily passing the best locations to stop for the night, or just to know that a little bit more would place me where I would get the maximum benefit from my gas stops.

Either way, seeing too the altitude displayed was most interesting. Altitude seemed a thrill to me, perhaps due to my prior life experience scaling so many mountains before falling to my death as George Herbert Leigh Mallory. This trip put me nicely in Amarillo, Texas one night when the air was brisk, the stars clear, and comfortably lodged in another La Quinta Inn. I awoke to snow though and I had been totally unaware of the pending storm. That storm stopped my forward momentum for three days as roads were clogged and snow equipment either in short supply or in use elsewhere. The interstate right next to the motel remained a barrier to my travel but a Denny's Restaurant stayed open and it was within walking distance if trudging through the snow drifts on foot to get there didn't deter you. My dog Sara seemed most upset by the snow—it was a new experience for this Florida raised pet.

Finally getting back on the road on the morning of the third day caused me some caution—there were still many patches of ice and snow, but the roads heading across Texas were fairly well tended and I looked forward to my arrival in Louisiana. I had called ahead and asked a friend, William Faulkner, Bill, to assist me when I arrived. He was a character all right, a friend and co-worker from the Customer Service Call Center who was about my age but wore his hair long and from time to time seemed under the influence, even perhaps at work. I did my best to ignore these times, preferring instead to share conversation with more people around us. We had our private conversations though and I knew that he loved his wife, and took care of a disabled adult child. Because we worked together, I took the time to advise him that he could get health insurance since he had none. Bill and I were hired in the same training class for work and spent the six weeks joking about life's trefoils and the challenges of just trying to keep our heads above water in a very, very challenging economy. I had more skills than Bill did, in fact I wondered how some people managed at all considering the limited opportunity in the area, and what was becoming an obvious downturn in the economy.

When I contacted Bill I really just wanted to see him again, one of the few friends I had in the area. Before leaving Louisiana, I had tried to give Bill some of my furniture but he missed out by missing several set appointments. The furniture went to a charity thrift shop as a result.

I knew his family could use the furniture but it does take a bit of self-motivation and motivation seemed lacking in Bill. We never could arrange an agreement for delivery that Bill would keep. Surprisingly, Bill showed up to meet me when I arrived at the storage unit. I was glad—it was only a few items to pick up, but a couple were heavy enough that the two of us made the job easier. And, all of the items were on the second floor and stairs was the only way down for the items. Bill helped me with those, and as we did we just chatted.

Bill confirmed something that I knew about the town, he saying "You know we have orgies here, right?" and I said "yes, I know." I didn't explain how I had come to know this fact since the local tradition is the town's big secret, but replied immediately that "I didn't want the karma."

It was actually the first time that someone had said directly what I already knew, but other things had made the practice very much a poorly kept secret. Bill went on to complain that he was not feeling well, that he had left the Customer Service Call Center since I left the town. He had been fired for some minor infraction and the greatest impact had been that his medications had stopped. Bill had pancreatic cancer, and that was a drag on his health, and he feared what the future held. "This cancer is going to kill me," he said, "I just don't know how much longer I can hold on." I quickly corrected him by saying "No, you are not dying of the cancer. You'll suffer a heart attack and it will occur on August 30th, or on the 31th at the latest. Bill, I'm so sorry," I added.

Bill looked at me wide-eyed but quietly dropped his eyes to the floor. "Don't worry about it, Bill. Death is not a problem. I've been to the other side and it is home. It is loving, caring, and everything will be fine. If you can do anything to prepare your family, try to do it right away."

Bill and I finished up the work with the last few items and I appreciated his assistance even though it appeared that his assistance may have tired him even more than I thought. We stood by the bed of my truck catching up on more gossip, and thinking about the future. We didn't discuss my prediction any further, but we both knew it was there. After a short while, I realized I really needed to get back on the road, and Bill needed to get back to his home for rest. I closed out my account with the storage facility as Bill drove down the road, the last time I saw him.

It neared Christmas when I got an email from Bill's wife. She had gained access to his eMail account and seeing several exchanges— the humorous kind—nothing too heavy or personal, and thought that she would let me know that he had passed. In return, I called Bill's wife as my cell phone still had his home, cell, and the cell number of his wife logged under his name. I expressed my condolences and asked more detail. I often forget my predictions but our conversation reminded me. I asked if he died of the pancreatic cancer, and her reply was "No, he died of a heart attack. Bill died on August 31st." The reply had an incredible impact and I suddenly realized that it was the very same information from Bill's wife that I had given to Bill the previous February.

I shared with her that Bill had known the future, and she confirmed that Bill had told her that I was capable of psychic prediction. A few minor predictions given Bill while we worked together had played out, but Bill's passing was certainly more significant. Bill's wife also gave to me the detail needed to access a web page with more detail about the funeral service, confirming his death on the 31st of August, an event occurring on the exact day as the prediction had foretold.

What has amazed me about these predictions of death was one fact—information confirming their accuracy has come back to me by one means or another. Except for my own father's health, of course, I was unfamiliar with the person given the prediction to the extent that I would be able to keep up with their lives. In all cases, my personal activity was such that I could not have kept up, but the Universe has allowed me to know the outcome anyway. It is not that we all don't die, we do, but to know the when of it all is the aspect of psychic phenomena that amazes.

Meditation is a valuable practice, allowing you to align yourself with God's will, to get answers to pressing concerns, or understanding the nature of the Universe, or even such seemingly minor concerns as the karmic interaction between you and your parents, your siblings, and those friends and lovers, or even that love of your life. The answer to your dream may be simply your vague recollection of the promise made to you by God before your incarnation, or it may be the burden of task you promised to complete in your promise to God before your incarnation.

Assuredly, your promise to God before your incarnation carries a much, much heavier weight than that promise you made to God hoping for the new job, the new house, the resolution of the problems that seemed irresolvable in your eyes. Your two-kneed promise made from the bottom of your heart in a pleading to God and forgotten almost as quickly as made, carries little weight relative to the pre-lifetime duties you carry at birth, which have set much of your life's events into motion. Karma is one of the many discoveries you may seek through meditation, a practice best done daily, and if that is not comfortable, then I suggest you do it twice each day.

Chapter Fourteen

The results of meditation can be astounding. You may carry a conscious message in your mind as you relax yourself, but it is often to the real question looming in your heart that will be the answer that is revealed to you. For that reason, the after effects of meditation are relaxing and peace-giving, causing such physical effects as the reduction of blood pressure and a definite decline in stress. Your daily activities are easier, your time more wisely used, your perceptions less alarming, and your interactions with others more easily handled.

There are too the results of your efforts that play out in ways that change your life in a very literal way. My meditation has allowed me to see the Voice of God, Metatron, to understand my relationship with my mother in this lifetime by knowing our previous interactions, and giving explanation to the more difficult relationship with my father.

Even an uncle's previous association was revealed, giving explanation to the dynamics of family today. Seeking to see the creation of souls gave me a glimpse of the Creator though from a time and perspective that was simply unexpected and not easily explained nor described.

My practice of meditation was intense in the latter 1980's when I sought to see the creation of souls. With the advice of Edgar Cayce, derived from his readings and reprinted in a variety of books by various authors and approved by the Association of Research and Enlightenment, Cayce's repository of readings in Virginia Beach, Virginia, I on a daily basis sought the contact with God afforded by meditation. As much to my delight as my surprise in the beginning, it worked! Surprise is no longer an element as wonderment has replaced surprise and the stream of enlightenment has never ceased. Meditation holds that key, and I recall reading where Cayce explained that it is wise to practice meditation in that the practice is both here on the earth plane and on the spirit plane. You will need to know, so why not gain the benefit of practice now?

If we were to strip away the day-to-day concerns that cloud our core purposes, wouldn't we do all we can to achieve as much spiritual progress now as we can? When we return to God, shouldn't we do so with progress and achievement rather than returning with unfinished business or less than stellar results? Karma is made of our efforts, karma being both good and bad. Let the pieces we assemble be as fine as we are capable of making.

Seeking to see the creation of souls was literally, unsuccessful. The reason I believe is that at the moment of creation, souls were not conscious. I did come into a vision though that gave me much of what I wanted: the sudden placement in the Universe—what appeared as if stars were spread out before me but knowing that the dots of light before me were each the same as me—a soul! There was a sensation or a knowledge of movement—a moving away from something that, with the purpose in mind for my meditation, allowed me to turn around. It was not a physical movement, it was a mental movement as I looked behind me and my forward direction unchanged as my view changed to where I had come from. What I saw was the most that I was capable of understanding at the moment. I saw God—the creator! As the source of all that existed, I saw for the first time my origin, my beginning. There in the center of a sea of souls moving away from the center was the Center, the Creator!

Made of the brightest light, an image that I could perceive was what appeared—a man with a crown, and a flowing robe, and made of dazzling stars, holding a scepter in his right hand. The feeling of love was overwhelming as I briefly peered and in that love was the push that was guiding me forward, well behind other souls, well before even more.

A moment later I seemed back in my body as I gasped a deep breath and my body heaved from its quiet state. I lay there in wonderment, pondering the experience, seeing again in visualization and with memory the image of God. I knew that I was one of only a few that had ever seen that image, and I would cherish it for all time. All of this because I had learned to meditate, and bore the curiosity that opened my eyes to Glory.

No less important was a meditation one day when I suddenly appeared—that is to say I was unaware of movement or direction and had no expectation—but quite literally as I lay on my bed reclining, then I was in front of the Voice of God, Metatron. No transition, no expectation, no sensation, just a sudden change from my reclining position to the place where I then came to exist: my reality had simply changed. Before me the form of Metatron.

Clear and unmistakable, the Voice spoke. "What are you doing here?" In reply I said "I don't know. I don't know who you are but I know that I work for you."

"What do you want", said Metatron, as I searched for an answer but could only say "nothing" in reply. Trying to add to my response, my words came awkwardly "I'm incarnate now, it has been a very strange life" thinking it seemed odd that I was explaining anything to Metatron, in that I inherently knew that He knew everything about everything, and everything certainly about me!

Here I stand, or at least the perception of standing. My field of view seemed to be all encompassing, but with a point of perspective that is not much different from what I experience each day in my earth bound life. I look out, I see, I hear, and with perhaps just a bit of higher detail in what I was looking at. Not a great difference, even nearly imperceptible. Before me though was Metatron, and I felt not small, but as a pinpoint of light before the greatness that was Metatron, and I was in my real skin. I was not changed, not embarrassed in any way and I knew that Metatron had seen me literally countless times as I now appeared before him. I could see Metatron, Metatron could see me, but I could not see me and there were no mirrors around to resolve that problem. In reality, I felt comfortable, at ease even, with this part of God before me.

This book, The Psychic Life of George Herbert Leigh Mallory, has to carry a burden in order to be accepted as I pray that it will be accepted. It must be the truth, as profound, as amazing, as out of bounds, as in left field as it might appear. Truth will always prevail whether on earth or as it is in heaven, to borrow a phrase. This book was not undertaken to be petty or to entertain—I could have easily written a book on the events of this lifetime, but it was my desire to explain to the world the events of my death as George Herbert Leigh Mallory on the eighth of June, 1924.

To give that information and to know that I speak honestly, frankly, and with the reality of that moment, I have to be just as honest and forthright now, with the many experiences I'm relating from my reincarnated lifetime. Why this preface to the just the next few paragraphs? I'm about to describe Metatron and to describe the course of events that followed my appearance before the Voice of God.

The form of Metatron is both familiar and unexpected. Seen in many logos, even on our money, and always in the natural expectation of those about us, Metatron is as "a great blue Eye into which blue electricity flows." Before me as I knew myself standing before the Voice of God, was an eye, all of blue, with the cornea all blue without an iris, and the shape of an eye without the "white of the eye" which was there in form but in color blue and slightly textured. At irregular intervals, long streams of "electricity" flowed into the eye mostly at the upper and lower left and right. It flowed slowly, as if having a life of its own, not like lightening, not like an inanimate something, more like a strand of energy.

It seemed as a child coming home—expected, welcomed, and clearly with a purpose. I did not ask, nor could I have diverted my thought and conversation to ask what the electricity was to Metatron. No, my energy was singularly held by and focused on my interaction with Metatron.

I asked "what is your name" and the reply was Metatron, of course, but I could not clearly understand His reply in my confusion. I thought the reply was Metronome, like the musical time or beat keeper. I repeated metronome two or three times and Metatron said "you will understand" and I ceased asking, relying on His wisdom that the question would be answered for me. It was only a short time later, a few days after the meditation that I saw the word Metatron and immediately realized the correct name for the Voice of God. An internet search confirmed that Metatron was the ancient Hebrew name for the Voice of God. My answer had come.

"Come with me" boomed the command and I realized that I was traveling with Metatron. While He moved, I moved with Him in perfect synchronicity—the field of view beyond and to the sides of Metatron changing and going by He and me but without a feeling of movement, or so I thought.

It was just an instant when I realized I had entered a different realm— Metatron firmly at the helm and me moving without conscious knowledge or the execution of will. I was just there, and Metatron led me and I went along in amazement. No fear, no curiosity, but a sense of wonderment and a new feeling—a feeling never previously experienced. The realm that we entered was, for lack of a better description, much like diving into the children's ball cage at a fast food restaurant. You probably know what I mean—the brightly colored, plastic balls that the very youngest of children play in without fear of suffocation.

Not small enough to be of danger and not heavy enough to do harm. That was what Metatron was leading me through right now—I felt as if atoms traveled along my back as we forged ahead but I had no back that I knew of in this state. There was a feeling too—a new feeling that I simply have no words to use to describe. A feeling that stirred my emotion pleasantly but without the deleterious affront of a drug. We continued, Metatron and I.

We seemingly burst from that world into an open sky as if into the space in between planets—black with stars, and streaming gases and Metatron directly in front of me as I whisked past objects beyond my belief and recognition or understanding. Again, another difference in feeling, a new emotion enveloped me and I took comfort in the fact that I was always exactly in the same relative position to Metatron. I had no fear, and only the slightest sensation of movement but my thoughts whirled with the passing of these sights and I felt protected.

There was a change in me that I have difficulty pinpointing—these journeys were more than a simple tour of parts of a vast universe, they were intended to effect a change in me that I could feel. Lacking a point of reference I could not hope to describe the change.

There is no doubt that many people incarnate or discarnate have experienced the same as I was then doing, but how could we share the wonderful news? What common understanding could we share?

As the journey continued Metatron and I then entered another dimension and I felt sluggish, perhaps even tired as I felt that I was pushing though a fog that inhibited my movement. Metatron was there in the same spot before me, but it was me having difficulty moving forward. I pushed I felt, but I really did not know what I was doing as each change in action, each glance about me seemed to bring about a different and unexpected result. I felt somewhat struggling but Metatron was there before me, all knowing, all seeing, and all that I had or needed to rely on as the journey continued.

It was just another moment as that very thought of the difficulty seemed to bring about a change again to my journey but this change brought a sense of overwhelming discomfort—not pain, not harm, but a sadness that quickly had me wanting to pull closer to Metatron.

My journey gave me new and unexpected sensations and just as quickly and without warning as I had entered the realm I found myself coming out of meditation. I slowly opened my eyes but lay on my bed in quiet comfort, reflecting on what had just happened.

Meditation is almost without exception a very relaxing process and this was no different. My breathing was slow and easy, my thoughts warm and my mind relaxed. I clearly remembered the events that had just passed before my eyes and I stared at the ceiling without focusing my eyes or even trying to see anything in particular.

Glancing at the clock did not occur to me though I usually tried to time my meditations—assigning a greater value to the longer meditations even if I could remember nothing that might have occurred. Those times lacking memory seemed very good to me—I always felt that the greatest amount of good had been done even though I could not tell you what had been done. My higher sense of accomplishment was always in play even if the slate seemed blank.

I was still stumbling with the name of the Voice of God as I lay quietly, thinking then still that it was metronome. Peace was the take home benefit of that experience, I thought. A warm and caring feeling that gives me comfort often.

The art of meditation is really a simple one—learning to both quiet the mind and to focus the attention all while holding a purpose or affirmation in mind. Simple enough, but it is practice that perfects, speeds, benefits, and ultimately rewards the practitioner with results. The desired result of daily practice is sometime obscured by a lacking of clear purpose, and the result often surprises. I have set off on whims only to be given weighty understanding, and at times there is not a clear division between the desired and the needed.

My thoughts one day asked for the karma that I was dealing with in this lifetime when I was given to view a scene that I knew to be Atlantis. I have spent two lifetimes in Atlantis, one some 200,000 years ago; the other only about 30,000 years ago—I was far more prominent in the latter incarnation and with power comes opportunity and ease to stray from God's Will for me. Questioning what I was dealing with in this lifetime I observed a place that would be described as a well designed Mediterranean villa, and somewhat of a sprawling one. The night's activity appeared to be a social event and the focus of the activity was an orgy.

I recognized myself—and as you meditate and as you seek answers you will know yourself and others not by their appearance but by the essence of their soul. This was a social setting—and there were others who I did not recognize and I understood that those persons are simply not incarnate at this time. The detail that came through was two-fold: I was dealing with the interaction of sex where it was appropriate meaning my purpose was loving and caring versus use as manipulation or the exercise of power. The other aspect was that my wife, who participated willingly in these affairs, was also the very loving soul that I would eventually meet again in this lifetime as Bobo where the extremes of duty would be pressed. What will we do for love? It does seem that the answer is almost anything!

I also observed my wife and I in our home—a strongly built home with thick walls, and a small bedroom with a high stacked bed. In the reception area as we entered was stark furniture—a settee that was round, with a backrest that rose up to provide a degree of comfort though far less that we would expect from contemporary design for furnishings. This furniture seemed more in place in a Victorian parlor setting than my meditative recollection of Atlantis. The walls were solid, the windows deep set and appearing to be without glass or other barrier. Atlantis was said to be in a very temperate climate according to the Cayce readings and window glass may simply have been unneeded. The images were clear but brief—the greatest impact of that meditation was the defining aspect of karma, and the abundance of love that carries lifetime to lifetime. Images in meditation can have profound effect on an individual—they have for me—and can change behavior and explain purpose in life.

This visit to Atlantis also gave insight to work and position as I realized that my function in that lifetime was as a director, or such similar position. As project director, I was being consulted though I did not recognize the souls, the persons, who were around me, and as I have discussed with others in the present day world who also are aware of their past lives, I have learned that seemingly few had lifetimes in Atlantis though my pool of information is absurdly small, to say the least. Clothing was interesting, but color selection would be well out of place for me in today's world.

The garb I wore at that time that I viewed was loose, functional, and characteristic more of Hollywood wardrobe than of something I might select from my closet today.

Starting at the feet, the shoes were simple sandals, flat without heels that I could discern, but strapped on in the manner of ancient Rome. Leather straps wrapped up the calve nearing the knee from both sides of the sandal. Somehow secured or tied just below the knee but above the calve, both straps appeared secure and felt (yes, you can get sensation and emotion from meditation) firm on the foot.

I wore a tunic as did those persons with whom I was conferring but all were different. We were not uniformed as there was variation across the clothing worn by the lot of us. My tunic was brown and white, with the brown used as trim around the neck, sleeves, and the hem. The neck was oddly squared off and the arms closer to the body but with a large openings about the point of the elbow. Synched at the waist, there continued a short but wide skirt that ended about mid-thigh. We would look at this type of clothing as being more theatrical today but then in Atlantis it served the purpose of modesty since climate demanded little of the wearer.

That meditation also revealed more points of interest. One was that I was the Director of the project—the project being the construction of a highway system to encircle the continent.

The second point addressed the long acknowledged aspect of superior technology believed to exist in Atlantis. As we were meeting we stood near a boat and shortly stepped onto that boat and continued conferring while standing on the bow area. As we stood easily there, the boat raised slightly above the water and moved forward towards the land across the bay or channel, whichever was the broad body of water in front of us. We moved swiftly, I could tell that, but I realized too that there was no impact of wind—we were protected by a force that both moved us and negated the buffering of the wind. The day was clear and the temperature comfortable. This was Atlantian technology, technology unknown today but well known then and generally used then. I know none of those persons today with whom I then conferred, my incarnation today relating more to family interactions than business associations.

Chapter Fifteen

Meditation can also provide resolution to current problems and may well do so with the most amazing of methods. In 1982 I purchased what I thought was my first gold—a box link necklace and bracelet that I recognized as the iconic necklace worn by Greek Gods. What a day! Too much Ouzo provided generously by the proprietors of the jewelry shop on Santorini, Greece, who, looking back, were not so concerned about the hospitality but were very concerned about changing the mental state of the customer.

I concede the problem was mine and I foolishly accepted the offer to imbibe while shopping but I was enthralled with the gold chain and in a state that seemed retrospectively anything but rational and calm. My first international trip, my first cruise, and my first gold in this foreign land—and an American Express card that would not limit my interest or my ability to buy all set before me set me up as an easy mark.

As I became the mark with my consumption and a few traveling companions milled about looking at the outrageously priced but exquisitely designed jewelry pieces here at Golden Santorini, I consumed more Ouzo and shortly just had to have the gold chain to hold and cherish—the cost be damned, and at that point, wasn't this a very special time in my life? The purchase was made and it could not be anything even remotely described as a wise purchase. No, I carried home some very, very expensive jewelry but the ship sailed, and I have never been back to Santorini. American Express doesn't forget though and soon after returning to the United States, the bill arrived to my great regret. Even more insulting was a ring with an emerald on it that was to be sized and sent to me—my trust and my American Express Card knew no bounds that day.

After struggling to pay for the purchase, I held onto the gold for years and still wear it today. There was a time though that I had to pawn the item in Kingsport, Tennessee as times had gotten tough again, and I needed the short term loan.

The year was 1989 and my luck for employment was anything but at a peak. I just could not seem to get a source of income. The pawn shop in the center of town provided the loan with the gold chain as collateral—a common everyday experience across the land and it came with simple terms: take the money offered and repay within 30 days with a small premium and the chain will be returned. Failing that, the pawn broker then forgives the loan but becomes owner of the collateral, the gold chain. Those 30 days loomed and I still had found no way to get an income, and the deadline passed without a means for me to retrieve my overpriced but endeared gold box link chain. After the end of the period though, the clouds parted and the sun broke through: I had at long last found employment. Not great, not wonderful, but employment none the less. I was a commissioned salesman for a small telecommunications company and the sale was fairly easy, and the commissions ongoing. I accumulated the money for retrieval but the time was closer to 60 days than 30, maybe even 90 days.

Once I had accumulated enough money for retrieval of my treasure, I visited the shop hoping for the best but was immediately disappointed. The pawn broker told me that my chain had been sold and he did have other items that I might like, of course. No, I thought, it was that chain that I wanted back—another did not have the history, the story to go along with it and there could be no substitution. I left the pawn shop dejected. Saddened by my failure and bad decision to let that be how this story was to end and how I could no longer have the classic Greek design to gracefully wrap my neck, I drove slowly home.

Meditation is never for the dejected though as it brings hope, peace, and even if nothing were to change I would at least feel better for having taken this brief time with God. So, meditation would be how I would deal with this loss.

At that time my daily objective was to meditate at the same time and in the same place each day, following what I had read of Edgar Cayce's suggestions and using the Edgar Cayce process.

Holding in mind my generic "To Be One With God" affirmation was not today's meditation. Today's meditation was "I want my chain back" more driven by disappointment than expectation. Much to my surprise there came a surprising revelation. That day I would learn something totally unexpected—I would learn that I have had gold before. Not in this lifetime perhaps, but surely in lifetimes past.

Much like the individual frames of a roll of film, "my chain" presented itself. One image followed by another image followed by another image presented itself. Each image different but each image a gold chain that I had owned—left from memory and consigned to the bin of a particular past life. One after another I said "no" and let the image pass. I held in mind the chain I had purchased in Greece and let pass from my fingers just in the most recent past. I did not know that there were many gold chains I had owned over time, but as each image flashed I recognized and for most part, let it pass without further concern.

One image gave regret though that I could not say "I'll take it (again!)" for it was most impressive and for some reason carries a fondness and definitely an authority. That gold chain symbolized some past life accomplishment where pride lay well, and honor to others was given. I wanted to say yes, but truth to my quest had me pass on this piece but it had now been brought back into the present day consciousness.

That chain had either five or seven significant parts—the center piece was a "half ball" laying flat again my chest which appeared perhaps 3 to 4 inches in diameter—significant weight for gold or any jewelry piece. It was flanked on both sides by two identical pieces of just slightly smaller proportions, and next to those again, a pattern repeat with just slight smaller "half balls". Two more smaller proportioned pieces touched the shoulder blade when worn.
I moved beyond that piece reluctantly even though my decision to do so was fast and immediate. A few more pieces flashed by before I suddenly realized that I had said "yes" and all of the images faded, and my meditation ended.

I had found and identified the piece I wanted returned, and I left it to the Universe to take care of my needs.

About six weeks later I was driving in downtown Kingsport and noticed that a new pawn shop had opened. Kingsport is in East Tennessee and the only real excitement is some 22 miles away at the Bristol Raceway—a NASCAR course that brings media attention to the area several times a year. Otherwise, the stench of the Eastman Chemical plant or Mead Paper wafting in the air is about all that moves your attention. The downtown main street, which used to be the area's cruising spot until town fathers sought to destroy the only enjoyable pastime for youth in the area by preventing certain traffic patterns, was lined with thrift and second hand stores now. The soda shop, the cinema, the 5 & 10 cent store, all now memories of the past. A new pawn shop? It is worth a visit, I thought.

Parking my car and walking in, I had forgotten my meditation about the chain but I by no means had forgotten the chain.

I asked the lady proprietor where gold chains were displayed, and she directed me to the glass case. Peering through the display case my eye immediately went to the box link chain and I asked to see it. Yes, this was the chain that I had pawned and it was here again!

The clasp is a manual clasp and the gold content is marked 58.5—in European fashion. In the United States we tend to see 14K but this was distinctive and this was mine. The price had gone up considerably but the Universe had prepared me for that—and I had just enough money to repurchase my item. One thing is sure, this gold chain has gotten expensive but at least I had it. I promptly bought the piece for a second time and I was out the door. This pawn shop was only a short distance from the first shop where the chain had been pawned and I was going to stop in to let the shopkeeper know of my good luck.

As I walked into the shop where I had originally pawned the chain, the clerk greeted me. I walked to stand in front of him and was about to share the information that I had retrieved my chain when a now familiar feeling overcame me and I felt the rush of words come forth: "You had an opportunity to tell the truth and chose not to. You disappointed when you could have encouraged, you deflected when you could have added clarity. You wanted to enhance yourself rather than benefit your fellow man. You chose a lie over the truth."

All of this came forth in a tone of voice that commanded attention and all of this cutting quickly to the core. I shuddered knowing that what was being said was not being said by me but would have an impact that would be definite and would leave a very lasting impression.

It was by no means the first time that I had channeled but each time is both amazing and surprising—God wants to make his point and I become the mouthpiece. It happens for many reasons. To correct an error as might be the case here, to instruct as has often happened in twelve-step meetings where the wisdom must be shared, with must being the operative word. And even more varied reasons.

I thought "the poor fellow!" I exited quickly surely leaving the man a mere puddle on the floor. My chain had been returned and God making sure that the moral fault had been made right. What had happened is that the owner of the first pawn shop had divorced the woman in the second pawn shop—she taking half of the inventory to her new business which included the chain I wanted returned. The man knew where the chain was but wasn't about to help his former partner-in-life, and now ex partner-in-business.

The meditation also gave me a new attitude regarding gold—never really thinking about it but finding a familiar comfort as the years went on. Though very particular in my selection criteria, I have accumulated a few pieces of exceptional design. The large necklace of "half-ball" design and construction hasn't materialized yet, but I always keep my eyes open. I've had it once, perhaps I can have it again.

Meditation can also be used to discover the karmic relations you are dealing with and there are surprising discoveries to be made. Taking my own family, and that part of the family that is slightly extended. I am amazed how people complain that their mother, or their father, or their sibling just drives them crazy when what is closer to the truth is that you—the complainer—had made the choice to incarnate to be placed precisely in the conditions and order that you now complain.

Is your father annoying? Did you not realize that you chose that very soul to be your father to be close to them? Most of us love our mothers with an incredible bond but you too chose them to be just that way—and for the children that think their mothers will drive them to pure insanity remember also that too is your challenge.

According to Edgar Cayce, all of the actions of the soul are recorded on the Akashic Records and meditation can unlock detail for you if you practice well and seek that information.

Remember too that it is the soul that is to be followed: don't be confused by the possibility of a change of sex, or relationship when considering the karma at play here. You are always born into the best circumstances for your spiritual development. Embrace the idea and rejoice with it—and be ready to carry the burden too.

Using meditation I have learned that my mother in this lifetime was certainly one of the souls with whom I had greatest desire to be close to while incarnate in this life. Loving and caring, I could always rely on her to be understanding and supportive, and certainly fair. While she did not always agree with me, when my mother did not agree with me I knew why—for whatever reason it might be.

I found my mother as the soul who was my wife in the period of about 1400 AD—the same lifetime I left by suicide. I believe strongly that I took my life as an "honor" resolution—having either allowed someone to escape my capture when I was responsible for their confinement either with intent or in error. The soul in this lifetime who was my mother was a radiant, loving person and I'm sure my departure left her heartbroken.

That same soul was also present in the period of 800 BC, where my mother was again my mother—a grand person was she, and I but a child of about 8 years. The setting here was Persian or somewhere near that region. A guard entrusted with her incarceration in that lifetime was the same soul who was my father in this lifetime—and I see clearly why we were all together again.

My father served my mother well in this lifetime having a reversal of fortune since he actively denied her care in that lifetime and my mother suffering from rheumatoid arthritis most of her lifetime just ended. My association in this lifetime served to allow my father to be in a position where I could find compassion and forgiveness for his acts in this lifetime—relieving also the pent up anger from that lifetime.

My biological father in that 800 BC lifetime was none other than an uncle I have today—and my relationship with my uncle has been stellar all this life. We obviously did well and were happy to be near each other again!

Confirming the continuation of life after death, as I slept at 2 AM in 1986, I was awakened to see my mother standing at the foot of my bed. She was very much at peacefully dressed and full bodied. Her hands fresh and open—a stark contrast to the ever bent, painful stubs that her disease had inflicted on her. In my lifetime she had become a small woman, bowed by the weight of pain and years, now again youthful as she stood there.

I was in Wilmington, Delaware, and she, in Eastern Tennessee confined to a nursing home due to her advanced state of arthritis. I knew immediately that she had passed from this earth but wanted to take a moment to say goodbye.

My mother always was spiritual, having given me the classic "Jonathan Livingston Seagull" to read years before. My father's call some 45 minutes later confirmed my loss—my mother had indeed passed. I did get to say goodbye with my few private words and my eyes stream now as I relate that memory and recall those feelings. I told my father that I knew she had gone, but he never did recall that event—I'm sure his own feelings were in play. His life partner, a soul mate to both of us, had passed too. We shared that connection.

Meditation provides other information and opportunities at times and enlightenment of very unusual nature. I have had two occasions of meeting someone in meditation, on the astral plane as it is often referred. The first was a young man, disabled and restricted to a wheel chair, and the son of a delightful woman in Kingsport who conducted classes in what is called "A Course in Miracles"—a somewhat formalized spiritual study, but a valid one. While the adults would sit around the table discussing the text and concept, the young man would sit awkwardly in the wheel chair attempting to hold his head upright while it bobbled.

He was one of those unfortunates whose lot in life will be to receive the care and help of others all of his life, however long that might be. The body does not provide opportunity for much more than mere existence and we often offered prayers for healing and enlightenment for this young man. This young man presented the first of my astral plane surprises though by meeting me on the astral plane one day. Deep into meditation, I turned my focus to see a mere speck approaching me with the long cord following—the silver cord. I've never come to know where that silver cord was connected, I can only guess or assume that it is connected to the person's body on the earth plane but remember, that is speculation.

As the speck approached and grew larger I recognized the young man and it was as if his face had been placed on the top of this piece of cord, onto a ball, and he smiled. I recalled that my reaction was to smile too— but an upturn of the lips and my face was probably not the outcome. This smile came from somewhere much deeper and it was a greeting of feelings rather than words or social connection. He was there for but a moment before turning and heading elsewhere, but I realized that he was not as much of a captive in his own body as we had all assumed.

On the earth plane, he gurgled, bobbled, and worked hard to communicate on any level, but here on the astral plane he moved easily and smiled from the bottom of a very, very large heart.

The next time we met for the "Course in Miracles" class, the young man made an especially difficult but successful effort to acknowledge our meeting. With the help of his mother, he and I acknowledged our meeting on the astral plane and the class was pleased not only in my efforts, which was to advance my meditative techniques, but in the confirmation that the young man was capable of moving much more than some of us had thought. It was not until that time that his mother had made any effort to let any member of the class know of this unusual experience which the young man apparently practiced on a regular basis. The time spent on earth by this young man was without the benefit of mobility that most of us enjoy, but even without that benefit, he had been given gifts beyond the comprehension of most of us.

Why he was physically restricted—through accident, defect of birth, or even karma—was never disclosed as we didn't discuss that leaving those questions out of polite conversation. The answer will be known, just not now.

The second time I encountered someone on the astral plane came in the year 2004, very much to my surprise not by the event, but by the person who contacted me. That person was George Walker Bush, the Supreme Court appointed person who was installed as the 43rd President of the United States.

As before and during meditation, my encounter with this person was unexpected and abrupt. The approaching entity was unknown to me in that it faced away until the top of the silver cord was immediately near me, and the face turned around as if to confront me.

The sneering face of George Bush was immediately in front of me and I felt immediately offended—I had no interest in having this person visit me then, or ever. In fact my response was a bit less than cordial or cultured. All I could do at the moment, and understand that responses on the other side offer no opportunity for refinement, was to say in a very demanding way "get out of here, you piece of shit." Perhaps not the most diplomatic way to say something, but certainly indicative of my evaluation of George Bush. A sneer came across his face, and he turned and left. I would like to say flee but I really feel that he came to tell me that he had something out for me.

Perhaps it was his intent to intimidate me, but I rely on God for my salvation. "My thoughts are as always, "what are you going to do about it, kill me? Is that your best shot?", knowing that when I do pass from this earth that it will be God before whom I stand, without concern or consequence of other souls who may demand their piece of flesh. There is but one standard of performance, and it is God's standard of performance. To any other soul I suggest making good use of the Wisdom of God, it is your guide, it is yours to use as the comparison for all of your thoughts and your actions. Toss away all of the other interpretations of God's will and use God's will. Nothing like relying on source material for a firm footing in reality, and reality is God.

Chapter Sixteen

So George Bush had gone, and I thought nothing more of it. This event was sometime in 2004 in the third or fourth quarter and no particular mind was paid to the event. My disregard should have been a bit more considered though as on the 15th of December, there was a change.

The runup to the housing bubble involved easy credit and builders were on a tear to get product out there and people into homes. My guides had given me a push—not so much direct instruction—but a compulsion to buy a house and they had directed me to an advertisement in the Miami Herald describing the new development Murano in Miramar, Florida designed and offered by Center Line Homes.

The week before the sales opportunity I took the trip to the construction area and the nearby sales office according to the directions provided in the paper itself. The distance seemed incredibly far away using the roads suggested, and I was not that familiar at all with Broward County and certainly not at all with Miramar, Florida. However, after leaving the sales office where I gathered some additional sales brochures and a layout of the development, I decided to follow my instincts to go home by what I thought might be an easier route. I was wowed to discover that the future construction site was only a short distance from my office location in Pembroke Park, and only a few hundred more feet from an entrance to Interstate 95. Wow! The place where my guides were sending me was very close to work, and easy to find! I looked forward with anticipation to the sales opportunity beginning the following week.

That next week passed quickly and I developed some second thoughts about making the purchase but drew myself to drive up to the sales office by mid-afternoon on Saturday anyway.

Arriving at the sales office I was surprised to find a long line waiting for attention and an opportunity to purchase and I wondered if this was a good idea. Still, I engaged myself with those waiting and the wisdom of buying now seemed more acceptable.

I had reviewed the models and learned the premiums associated with buying in certain areas of the development-to-be, and had rejected some ideas. There was a $10,000 premium associated with being lake-front, a small manmade lake that centered the development of 196 townhomes. I thought the cost to be excessive and had selected a certain model of two master suites as my target, but a bit out of the way in the back of the development. The back of the development, I reasoned, would reduce traffic and that pleased me. The sales office bustled with more than enough sales staff and I was quickly seated and almost to the point, the sales person just asked me which unit I wanted. I pointed out my unit, and was quickly told that the unit was not available. However, a similar unit was available lakeside, he related. No, was my reply, I premium of $10,000 was too much and I wanted to either decline or find the same unit elsewhere.

The salesman quickly conferred with his manager and offered to reduce the premium to $5,000. I thought well of that knowing that a resale would benefit me, and $5,000 was not much for "water front" a favorite term in South Florida.

We agreed, and on May 3, 2003, I signed the documents and gave over a substantial check to hold my purchase. The check was refundable if I were to be unable to secure a mortgage for my purchase.

Fast forward to my walk through, just two days before my closing. A friend, Joe Roman, and I were doing the walkthrough on December 15, 2004 when my cell phone rang and the caller identified herself as an agent of the Secret Service.

"You have been identified as someone who might be able to help us with an investigation", the caller said, "can we meet you today."

My reply was "of course" but I told her I was away from my office but would be returning soon. "Would you wait outside until I arrive?"

I asked, I don't want you entering the office. "Of course", she replied, and we ended the conversation, promising to meet in just a few minutes.

My friend, Joe, and I completed the walkthrough and parted company, and I headed for my office. My arrival there didn't find the Secret Service agent, so I waited a few minutes before going into the office. The Secret Service agent and her partner were inside I was told as I entered, and the Director of the facility and the agents were waiting in the Director's office.

"My, exactly the scenario I had no interest in addressing—why could they not simply have done as asked", I wondered. OK, I conceded, time to meet the Secret Service to assist them in their investigation. Much to my surprise, I was the subject, not the assistance needed for their investigation.

After a few awkward exchanges we all sat and I reminded them that I had asked them to meet me outside, as I apologized to my Director for having the Secret Service show up at my office. Now, what did they want?

One agent pulled an email from his valise that was encased in a plastic sleeve and he held it carefully by the edge as he passed it to me. I realized immediately that the method employed to pass the memo was intended to have me grasp the sleeve in a manner that would provide my fingerprints for the agents without having to take a legal course of action to get my fingerprints.

I am an honest person, and I really had no concern either about the Secret Service having my fingerprints. In fact, the government has had my fingerprints since 1966 when at the age of 18, I had been hired as a Civilian Dispatcher for the Bensalem Township Police Department. That would be a 911 operator in today's parlance.

Fingerprinting was standard, and someone at Homeland Security had not only my fingerprints but a current photo too as I had security clearance for the Port of Miami and Port Everglades both as part of my job related duties. This was only three years into the post 9/11 world.

I took the eMail and read it through the plastic. It was my eMail and the destination was <u>President@WhiteHouse.Gov</u>, the eMail for George Walker Bush, the appointed but unwarranted President of the United States.

The content was short and to the point: "I pray that you come to know the pain and suffering that you have caused the people of Iraq."

That's it, nothing too much, a valid sentiment sent in response to George Walker Bush having somehow reached a conclusion that Iraq was somehow involved in the attacks on the World Trade Center on September 11, 2001. Iraq was not, we know that, and we still lack a valid justification for attacking Iraq.

What, George, did the innocent people of Iraq do to justify their loss of life and destruction of their property other than to satisfy your insufficient ego, I still wonder.

In fact, I'm going to pose another question to you, George, on behalf of Cindy Sheehan, who you have tried to evade since she tried to question you on your motivation.

That question is this:

"What, George, was that noble cause for the war in Iraq you referenced referring to the death of Cindy Sheehan's son in that country?"

If you found such a cause, a noble cause, the answer should roll off your tongue easily. Since that answer has never been published, never been described, and the deaths of thousands of American and International Coalition troops have waited for the justification of war, I am sure George that you would like to set our moral angst to rest. The people of Iraq wait your reply too.

The meeting with the Secret Service lasted only a few more minutes and it was awkward—they trying to insist that somehow I had threatened the President, and me reminding them that my memo was a prayer. "I pray" it read, and it was a prayer, and no one, most definitely not the Secret Service, was going to tell me what to pray.

No, I was not a threat to the President any more than truth is, and the Secret Service hasn't yet tried to arrest the truth, have they? Well, no more than their attempts to hide the truth, which seems the greater threat to the country than my prayer for George Bush to know the extent of the damage he levied on the people of Iraq.

I gave no more thought to this encounter after the first few days during which my Director seemed intent to apply some scourging blame on me for the Secret Service showing up at his facility. I reminded the Director what the Secret Service had told me, and emphasized that the Secret Service had been asked only to meet me in the parking lot. I asked them to do that, not to enter my offices. Oh yes, the eMail came from my private account, not a business account so that issue was set aside.

The Secret Service didn't forget though, and without appointment or warning, the Secret Service has two different agents knock at my door one evening a few weeks later. My home was new, and the two men at the door were well dressed, and I saw no danger so I opened the door and they identified themselves as Secret Service Agents by showing me their identification and badges. Asking if they could come in to continue the discussion, I acquiesced, and allowed them entry. It was a very general discussion and I thought them a bit nosy but took the time to be polite. I had done nothing wrong after all, and had no concerns. Maybe, just maybe, they actually had a valid reason for being here but as the visit dragged on, I saw less reason for their presence.

One person seemed to play the "good cop", the other played the "bad cop" but they both became annoying and after an hour or two I asked them to leave. They did, and I thought finally this annoyance was complete. They kept trying to tell me that I had threatened the President, I kept reminding them that I had not.

A second visit a few weeks later by the same two agents who had last visited was also unannounced and the roles were the same for the "good cop" and the "bad cop".

Frankly, their visit was simply taking my time without benefit to either of us—they both seemed intent on convincing me that I had done something wrong and that I was threatening the President but I would have none of it.

They grew a bit frustrated and I became more annoyed but I remained resolute and polite. After a period, I asked if there was anything that they were here to give to me since I had no interest in giving anything to them, and getting no answer, asked them again to leave. I decided at that time either to not answer the door if they showed up again or certainly, not to invite them into my home.

The need for an invitation was swiftly swept aside on their next visit. Sitting in the family room of my home with the sliding glass doors overlooking the waterfront view and a bowl of ice cream on my lap, SWAT Team uniformed officers stepped from both the left and right views to my utter amazement. That action was not what I expected when I sat down to eat ice cream and watch television, and it was a decidedly unnerving view.

It was now June 2005, and I had pleasantly stopped thinking about the Secret Service. The two men on the opposite side of the glass pointed to me and indicated that I should answer the front door. I set down the ice cream and walked briskly to the front of the townhome. As I swung open the front door, a cadre of police officers from the local force, the state police force, and headed by the two Secret Service agents, accompanied by more Secret Service agents stood there. Many were armed and same had their guns drawn.

My composure was easy though and I said simply "Do you have a warrant?" knowing that access to my home can be denied unless a court order for entry had been issued. The Secret Service agent answered "yes" and held up a piece of paper. My reply was classic in its spontaneity and grace.

"Well then, as afforded under the provisions of the Constitution of the United States regarding unreasonable search and seizure, you have gained the approval of a Court of Law to gain entry. Gentlemen, come in!" as I swung the door back and invited everyone to come in.

AO 93 (Rev. 5/85) Search Warrant

United States District Court

SOUTHERN DISTRICT OF FLORIDA

In the Matter of the Search of
(Name, address or brief description of person or property to be searched)

Residence located at 8371 S.W. 29th Street, Miramar,
FL 33025 for computer(s), computer hardware, software,
computer-related documentation, computer passwords
and data security devices, any computer or electronic
records, electronic storage device, and non electronic
records relating to the operation of computer(s), and
maintenance of any internet service provider account(s).

SEARCH WARRANT

CASE NUMBER: 05 - 2790 c M 7

TO: Special Agent Jeffrey Nickols, USSS and any Authorized Officer of the United States

Affidavit(s) having been made before me by Special Agent Jeffrey Nickols, USSS who has reason to
believe that ☐ on the person of or ☒ on the premises known as (name, description and/or location)

SEE ATTACHMENT A

in the District of there is now
concealed a certain person or property, namely (describe the person or property)

SEE ATTACHMENT B

I am satisfied that the affidavit(s) and any record testimony establish probable cause to believe that the person or property
so described is now concealed on the person or premises above-described and establish grounds for the issuance of this
warrant.

YOU ARE HEREBY COMMANDED to search on or before JUNE 25, 2005
                                                            Date
(not to exceed 10 days) the person or place named above for the person or property specified, serving this warrant and
making the search (in the daytime -- 6:00 A.M. to 10:00 P.M.) (at any time in the day or night as I find reasonable cause
has been established) and if the person or property be found there to seize same, leaving a copy of this warrant and
receipt for the person or property taken, and prepare a written inventory of the person or property seized and promptly
return this warrant to DUTY MAGISTRATE JUDGE as required by law.
                        U.S. Judge or Magistrate Judge

JUNE 15 2005 5:05 PM   at   Miami, Florida
Date and Time Issued   City and State

Chris M. McAliley
United States Magistrate Judge
Name and Title of Judicial Officer   Signature of Judicial Officer

This form was electronically produced by Elite Federal Forms, Inc.

The first Secret Service agent handed me the warrant for a moment, then took it back and we reviewed it later. I wanted to make sure that approval had been granted-that the warrant bore what thought it should to afford the unexpected and legally required ability to enter my home.

I was bare-chested and the agents did not allow me to put on a shirt at that time, and I was led back to the family room where I picked up my bowl of melting ice cream.

The agents sat across from me on another sofa—the two sofas set opposite each other for easy conversation. The agents went on to ask if I had any weapons in my home, and I replied that I had kitchen knives, hand tools, but little else that would be construed weapons.

Upstairs I heard a search going on, with loud thumps and bumps but little else. I discovered later that they had entered the attic, had tossed the mattresses from the bed, and gone through every closet. In the end, only the computer and a stack of disks had were removed by the agents. The computer seemed logical, but the stack of discs were simply music mixes prepared on a disc jockey mix deck and recorded onto computer discs for review.

I did the mixes often as a hobby and to keep my skills sharp between performances or gigs for small groups or parties. I had long ago given up hope for a club gig even though my skill level easily met the criteria, but my age excluded me from real consideration. I am no longer a spring chicken, even in my own eyes.

The agents gave me a receipt for the items they thought should provide a case against me for prosecution for what they, not I, considered threats against George Walker Bush, pretender to the Presidency of the United States of America.

As a servant to God, I know that He, God, protects me and I was sincerely unconcerned about the overall outcome of this raid but did wonder how much trouble I would be put through before the inconvenience subsided. It was not that much later that the Secret Service left with their booty and I was left to straighten up the house.

Unlike depictions on television, the raid did not leave a trail of broken items and debris. No, a short time taken to remake beds and straighten items on shelves was about all it would take. The Secret Service promised return of my items within seven days. They took seven months despite my regular calls to their office asking for return of the items.

They might feel that they had reason to raid me for unfounded threats against the Office of President, but they had nothing to rely on other than to take action for me calling repeatedly to get my computer and discs back.

After about a month, I resigned myself to replacing the computer and delighted myself in buying a faster, certainly more up-to-date model. My, God does work in mysterious ways!

Chapter Seventeen

The connection I have with George Walker Bush is not from this encounter. No, my first mention of George Walker Bush was in the prophesy given me about fifteen months before the events of September 11, 2001. My neighbor and friend, Mark Carpenter, now of Southwest Florida but a neighbor one floor below me in the year 2000 in Miami, was with me on my balcony overlooking Biscayne Bay when a vision filled my head and I immediately stated the details of that event that was yet to come.

As if I were positioned directly above one of the towers of the World Trade Center, I observed the dust cloud being created that would engulf the streets of New York on the future fateful day.

My first words to Mark were "I don't know why, but they are taking down the World Trade Center. That is odd, it was only built in the mid-1960's. It is going to happen in late summer, early fall."

Mark stood back surprised as I continued. "George Bush is directly involved." The images in my mind showed me nothing of the catastrophe that surrounded the event, no, my vision was focused on the unemotional factual aspect and offered no explanation as to a why or wherefore, just addressing the what and the who. I got no understanding beyond that stated as to why George Bush was involved, I just know that he was and I know that he was directly involved. The prophesy of the World Trade Center came dramatically and tragically true and I still wonder the extent of George Walker Bush's involvement.

Visions are like a quick glimpse at a television screen. The sight can be confusing because they give an immediate view of an event without the run-up to the event or the opportunity to gaze further down the time line to see outcomes or effects.

Mark and I discussed the vision briefly, and I did my best to explain all that I had seen, but without reference points the information could only be given and accepted. There was not much more to be done and reading into the event distorts what might be gained from the information.

Even as late as September 2011, a psychic reading given me by a reader, and a reading given a friend by the same psychic reader at a separate time at a separate location both resulted in a warnings of an earthquake to occur in the area of Palm Springs, California in January 2012.

We both noted the event and watched for it to occur, preparing as much as was prudent or possible. The outcome was a bit different than either of the two of us expected.

There was an event, and that event was a wind storm. Sudden and without warning, wind roared down the canyons in Palm Springs, knocking over car ports, palm trees, and all things unsecured, and tearing fences from their footings. The scene suggested devastation and that was what had been seen by the psychic—it looked like an earthquake, but had in fact been caused by a very, very strong wind.

This is a momentary glimpse in time for sure, but with interpretation that stepped away from the eventual reality of the event. This is the problem with visions, particularly one or perhaps two, but lacking ongoing information it is simply difficult to be so sure of the future in all respects.

While I was right about the destruction of the World Trade Center Tower, I did not see the second tower being destroyed and that also occurred as we know. I did not see the full nature of the involvement of George Bush but I still have my gut feeling, and that gut feeling remains to this day. I know, but I don't have a leg to stand on, if you will, and my feeling is grave. Perhaps to the grave is where I'll eventually have to take my gut feeling on the subject.

Other prophesy has been given and at times the place, the person and the reason is all there initially but sometimes that is all you get, being left to fill in the blanks as time unfolds.

Another friend, Joe Roman of Fort Lauderdale, Florida was with me on a bright day on Lincoln Road in Miami Beach when I received a calling, an urging, to deliver a message for God.

Follow the Urge could be the message given me, but in truth there is almost an unrecognizable push to do something that is really at the heart of something like this. My friend Joe was probably very surprised when I pointed a finger in a direction along Lincoln Road that day, pointing to a person who was so far away that even height was almost indistinguishable above the horizon of the paved open space that is Lincoln Road.

I just knew that in that direction was where I was to walk and I picked up the pace with a brisk stride. Joe was right behind me, keeping pace but probably wondering where I was leading him. We took several long strides and we settled into a cadence of footsteps, a small group of men approaching and getting larger as the distance between us grew shorter. I stopped suddenly in front of my objective, a man who was quite a bit taller than me, a man who smiled and bent forward to hear me when I said I had a message for him.

"I have a message for you from God," the delivery started, "you are going to have an opportunity to be on television. Make that the full focus of your attention and it will set the tone and the direction for your career for the rest of your life." Then I went on to add "I don't say this often, but you are certainly a handsome man. Are you a Pisces" I questioned.

No was his reply, "I'm a Libra" but I seemed to have caught him by surprise. The handsome young man was tall, I'm guessing somewhere between 6'2" and 6'4", but from my short 5'6" he was a tall one from my perspective.

The meeting was awkward anyway—me walking up to someone on the street and letting that person know their future and claiming the information to a message from God. I don't think my friend Joe caught all that I was saying and having delivered my message, I didn't want to hang around.

As soon as my message was delivered, I politely excused myself and Joe and I walked briskly off on down Lincoln Road towards the parking lot where my car was near Meridian. I didn't ask the name of the message recipient—I just wanted to exit the scene as quickly as I could.

It may have been a year later when I was watching television and a new show was coming on. That new show was on the Home and Garden Network, better known as HGTV. The show was the first season of a design competition called Design Star and I was watching the young man on television who I had come across that day on Lincoln Road. His name is David Bromstad.

The person who received the message about his future was David Bromstad who did go on to win the first season's competition and has now compiled an impressive portfolio of quality programming with his Color Splash, then Color Splash:Miami shows, and now is even the mentor on the latest incarnation of the Design Star competition on the network. David is getting well recognized in his field, and is a staple on the network. I have written David both at his penthouse on South Beach (at least what I believe to be his address there) and also attempted to reach him through the network, but I have not been able to get his confirmation of the meeting. No worry.

My friend Joe remembers the occasion, as do I. And the prophesy of his well deserved rise to fame has been, hem, hem, spot on accurate.

I really can't take credit you realize, for if it were not the message that is the importance of the delivery, there would be no importance at all. It is the message from God that is significant, not the fact that I willingly serve God as and when he asks. If I'm to be repaid for any expenditure, if I am to be acknowledged, God will do all. This book I suspect is part of that recognition and that repayment—the concepts have flowed well and easily, and whether delivered in a flash of vision, or the belching of words to someone on the street, or the flow of words onto a computer screen, God gives back. Often as I have written the phrases that describe the experiences allowed me by God, by my spirit guides too, tears have welled up in my eyes but the reward is how quickly my fingers fly across the keyboard and something sensible to me, perhaps even astonishing to me, ends up in this story.

God does certainly have a sense of humor, a fact and realization we should all know and understand. Sometimes it is the speed that false beliefs are shattered. One such example occurred in that Central Louisiana town just a short time after I arrived there. Curious about a store, a store that apparently tried to come across as a top-end retailer, I stepped in to see who or what my local businesses were. The name of the store was straightforward with a large sign on the building naming it Trotter's Electronics And Appliances. I walked around, looked, and having moved from the very bustling area of South Florida with its trend setting, over-the-top designers (one being David Bromstad, who I just mentioned), I was not particularly impressed with the goods on display, but even so, did not mention that fact.

Not wise to render judgment, I'm new here, the outsider, and it was more important to make friends while I sought out where I might shop in the future. I am a long-term subscriber to Consumer Reports, a magazine I renew in five year increments so my eye is open to the products they recommend. After all, I buy the magazine for their recommendations, so why shouldn't I use those recommendations? Every product I have ever purchased relying on the Consumer Report recommendations has been more than satisfying, so a little research with the magazine is my real first stop before making a purchase.

I was not in the market for anything, but just looking about. There was a very nice gentleman who stepped up to offer me assistance and I let him know nicely that my presence was really just a look-see, I had no need and no intent for any product, but I was new to the area. We chatted for a bit about much of nothing—the casual conversation one usually has where conversation is necessary but not necessarily desired. I said I was new to the area and related the fact that I had seen the faces of the people that I was to meet here shortly before leaving Miami.

He stopped abruptly and said something to the effect that no one but God can do prophesy, and I countered him by saying that I had, that I was not God, so he had to be wrong in his statement.

"Well, tell me something then" he says, and my reply was "try this on for size." This was May of 2008, and the first step on what has come to be my odyssey from one coast of the United States to the other. "There will be an earthquake over 7.2 magnitude in China within three to six weeks. Thousands will die."

He looked at me funny, me surprising him with the prediction I suppose. There is not much that any person can say directly in response to prophesy—there may be questions to explain the prophesy—but this was direct. A date range, a description of severity, and location came in those few words I had given the clerk, and since it was in the future, it was prophesy. The conversation ended coldly but politely, and I left the store.

It was just a couple of weeks later when the news of the event came across the Cable News Network (CNN). There had been an earthquake in China, and it was in the 7.9 magnitude range, and there were thousands feared dead. Mass destruction was feared and the world watched as the events unfolded. My prophesy did not immediately leap to mind as I followed the unfolding events on television as I had done so often before. I recall the terrible unfolding events of the attack on the World Trade Center in 2001.

And I recall another event in 2007, which I'll relate shortly.

The salesman, Jimmy Logsdon, was at work the next time I stopped in. He greeted me professionally and I asked him if he remembered me and he said yes. I asked him too if he remembered the prophesy of the earthquake I had made and he looked at me funny before remembering the details of the event as predicted. He scowled a bit, and I realized what the problem was. It was not so much that I had accurately made a prediction, no, that was known and being relatively recent, memory was clear enough for easy recall. The problem was that an accurate prediction was contrary to the religious thought that "only God can do prophesy." I don't disagree that only God can do prophesy, the problem is that there are actually many people incarnate who have the ability to deliver that message for God. Much like the admonition that "when a teacher is needed, a teacher will come." We need to see people for who they are and set aside baseless assumptions. What God will have us do is often surprising, very surprising, and events of this nature are not that unusual. For me, even though I asked my guides to set back and let me forge on my own this lifetime, at least until this latter part of my life, many others very capable and still in touch with the other side have been introduced to me. I've always listened, and I've always weighed what was said with sharp consideration.

While I say listen to those about you, I am not saying that all those about you would do you well. No, there are many, many out there who would seek to benefit themselves. That is a problem I have encountered to my dismay. While I think the best of those who would help, the wolf in lamb's clothing can be found everywhere. Compare your base feelings with the standard you hold for God. Remember, you may make mistakes, but your karmic debt is only for those mistakes and actions taken which you do to enhance yourself. Honest errors carry no karmic weight if your intent is God-driven to begin with.

Chapter Eighteen

There is no misunderstanding on my part that God drives me to many of these encounters as He did in December 2003. As a Cruise Line employee, I did get cruising privileges and they are literally opportunities that I might ask for weeks or months in advance, but would get confirmation sometimes as late as the day before. For some, confirmations might be the day of the cruise but I have never been put into that position so I cannot speak from experience. The whole experience of cruising is just simply wonderful and draws people wanting to cruise from a broad spectrum of the population. Some of those people, like the next encounter I need to describe, come from the Halls of Congress.

It was December 2003 and I had been booked for the Christmas Cruise departing Miami on the 22nd. It was a last minute opportunity for me and I had sailed the Navigator of the Seas before and it is an awesomely great ship. I've never been disappointed except once in my career—I invited a friend, a dear named Shirley Carter to sail with me but I could not get confirmed with my own cruise line. I was overly optimistic to expect a summer cruise confirmation but Shirley wanted to go and I was doing my best. There was no opportunity to get confirmed, so I did something unusual for me: that was to request a cabin on a competing cruise line. The cruise lines extend that privilege to each other, but it is generally hard to get confirmed that way, they too are confirmed late and the price is higher too. Not wanting to disappoint my friend, I requested a cabin on the now defunct Majesty Cruise Line. It was a bit of a step down, but coming from an industry leader to a "wanna-be" can eye-opening if nothing else. Our cabin was old—not small, but with two small port holes, and more indicative of the merchant marine than of a luxury cruise vessel. The cruise was fun because Shirley was there but we both realized that it did not come close to the quality of a cruise that we had hoped for and nothing compared to my sailing now on the Navigator of the Seas.

I am happy to say that even though Shirley was not able to sail with me again, I had her travel with my family on a later cruise where she got the opportunity to experience the full benefit of one of the world's best cruise lines on one of the world's best cruise ships.

That was the experience I now expected for my Christmas Cruise. My confirmation had to be one of those resulting from a last minute cancellation or something similar. A Christmas Cruise is highly desirable—the family enjoys a full range of on-board and port-of-call experiences, sumptuous meals and top notch entertainment and activities.

It is a package purchased, and a package enjoyed, and no one has to make even a bed. Having been with the Cruise Line for a number of years I had seniority and loving to cruise, that gave me a real advantage. It did pay to stick around and to work hard and I thoroughly enjoyed my work, and I enjoyed the people I worked with.

I don't recall which night of the cruise it was, but it was near the beginning of this seven night experience when I walked up behind someone who looked familiar. I recall what I said, but I have to also acknowledge that the introduction was not mine. The words gushed, the right words.

The way the words formed and the way the words came forward told me that the "other side" was doing the introduction and I had little opportunity but to go along for the ride.

"I have a bone to pick with you" I/they said. And the man in front of me turned to look quickly and I realized who it was. We had left the Port of Miami so finding a fellow Floridian was not a surprise but finding the person to be United States Senator Bob Graham was surprising. I stepped back a foot as if to give him room as he turned, and he said "OK, we can set up a meeting." I was floored by the surprise of the response, both by the fact that I had approached the Senator so brazenly, and perhaps too, by the ready acceptance of the request.

I gave the Senator my name, and my cabin number. The cabin number is the same as the telephone number so in doing so, I made contact between us easy. He promised to call me within a couple of days and I thanked him.

The call from the Senator came in just that time, and when it arrived I recall that it might have been 10 AM for a 2 PM meeting. Memory is fuzzy on this point, but what I was surprised most about was that the Senator had arranged the meeting for Deck 2 in the Conference Center. The ships of the fleet are very multipurpose, accommodating all sorts of consumer interests from rock climbing on the upper deck to ice skating down below.

Too, there are professional accommodations beyond cabins, to include conference rooms and meeting rooms. The Senator had secured the Conference Center and it was truthfully the first time that I recalled having visited one, even though I had given tours of these magnificent ships on many occasions. My function was usually tours for travel agents, or perhaps seminars at sea for similar groups, but the conference room was usually the domain of the business group which usually was conducted by the members of what was called Incentive Sales. That group handled special groups, full and partial ship charters, and the like. The visit to the conference center was impressive even to me. The special lighting and muted colors of this area added a certain distinction that was meant to impress—and impress it did.

As I walked into the room, there at the head of the conference table sat the Senator, with an array of items set out in front of him. There was no one else but the Senator in the room. He looked up and said "Well, you're on time" and my reply was spontaneous and direct "I am meeting with one of the 120 most powerful men in the world", a reply that surprised me for having said it. It was on mark, but even so, more direct than I would have liked or certainly planned. I walked briskly to my seat. I chose the chair right next to the Senator on his left, a seat that faced the Senator comfortably and allowed a relaxed, non-confrontational position to discuss my "bone" that I wanted to pick with the Senator. I didn't really have a full agenda—that was the prerogative of the other side. They brought me here, and I was just happy doing my service.

This was not the first Senator I have had the pleasure of meeting. A number of years earlier, I met Senator Hubert Humphrey, as we both exited the Kentucky Derby—each trying for that secret exit that would allow a quick departure after the race had ended. I recall that he was with a small entourage of handlers—men in suits—as he walked from the fence area of the park, and I just walked up as if I had known him for years and said "Hello, Senator, nice to see you." For me as a relatively young college student, I was impressed.

Too, I met Frank Rizzo and Bill Green on separate occasions. Both were at one time the mayor of Philadelphia, and Bill Green was in the area of Bristol, Bucks County, when I met him in a hotel lobby, but Frank Rizzo was somewhere in South Philadelphia, when I and my friends chanced upon him.

This was the first arranged meeting with any politically elected person though, and I relied on the "other side" to guide me as I could not think of anything that I was to talk about.

Being the messenger does give me some unusual opportunities though and I was ready to take that opportunity. It was right to the point from there—I wanted to speak to the Senator about immigration. The census had taken place only three years earlier and the results of the census seem to take forever to come to light and they come out piecemeal at best. The bottom line of the Census 2000 was that the United States of America had grown in population by about 32 million persons, a ten percent increase and some 60 per cent of that increase was fueled by immigration.

I am greatly disturbed by our lack of efforts to stem that growth, and in light of today's debate about illegal immigration, my subject matter was certainly one that should have been more directly pursued. The Senator stopped me almost immediately when I wanted to discuss immigration, so I put that subject away. Still, this was a meeting with a Senator and it was not to be wasted.

I moved onto the next topic of discussion—American infrastructure. I said to the Senator, "every presidential candidate for as long as I can remember has promised to address the issue but the fact of the matter is that no one has done anything. And this, Senator, I have to add" . . . my voice no longer was mine but out came the words that floated in the room, and recorded onto the device that the Senator had before him. "There will be a bridge collapse on Interstate 35 in Minneapolis, and there will be as many as 35 persons to die. The event will occur sometime between 2005 and 2007."

I was shocked that such detail should come before the Senator but there was nothing I could do about it. The voice may not sound differently to anyone else, but I can tell when the words are not mine. If to show where the detail comes from, I frequently use the term "belching" to describe both the source and the delivery of the information.

Whatever is being said is being said and I have no means to stop it. Like a water hose, I am a conduit for the information but also like a water hose, I don't know what is coming until it is there.

The Senator made a couple of quick notes and I readied myself to leave the room. I had failed in my quest to effect a policy change on immigration, and had even went well overboard on mentioning that the American infrastructure was deteriorating, and I did so in a dramatic prophetic manner. The Senator jotted down something on a piece of paper and handed it to me as I stood up. Not even a name, just an email address. That email address was ernestr@mindspring.com.

It has been a long time since that meeting, and I wasn't planning this novel then but given the few possible options for this, I do want to include the information. I've checked and the eMail is no longer functioning.

"Let me know if anything further was to happen", Senator Graham added.

The piece of paper I carried with me and I held onto another item too—the business card of United States Senator Bob Graham of Florida.

I had done my work, I assumed, and though I saw the Senator perhaps another time or two while on the cruise, we didn't stop to talk for long, nodding a polite acknowledgement as we passed. Much like ships in the night.

The future event described to the Senator—the Interstate 35 Bridge collapse came to pass in 2007 in Minneapolis and it made national news and brought even more attention to the state of American infrastructure.

As to the collapse, I have tried to get some additional information to those who are responsible for the maintenance of the bridge—I just want to tell them that a change in procedure that did occur in 2005 was the trigger for the calamity. My efforts to let someone know have been unsuccessful. I would like to tell you more of what that change was if I knew but perhaps simply by providing the year that the problem began might allow you to discern which particular maintenance items set the collapse into motion. This book may have afforded me that opportunity that I could not secure myself.

We are not taking care of America. We have failed to address the sanctity of the American Citizen by failing to exclude those who have invaded our country to take the land, the opportunity, the education, the health care, and the social support as if it were their own, all while failing to provide or contribute to those elements. This justification is beyond me—the seats of power are trying to wring out an extra measure of what they deem success by paying less for the labor of those who come here for opportunity. That grab for opportunity, unabated by the laws set into place to prevent such access to our land, may exist for a short period but is being destroyed for those whose right to be here is paramount.

Government has a purpose, we must realize, and that purpose is serve the Citizens who create it. There is no other balance in the world—all other acts cause an imbalance for mankind. Whether dictators or regimes, all efforts to bring the energy of the people to focus on the support of those who both govern and consume, will fail as those very people will be drained of the ability to uphold those who self-serve.

Chapter Nineteen

Now to a phenomena known as aura—the radiant light of the soul. Each of God's creation shines as brightly as the Father Creator as each is part of the whole, seeking but the return to join the Father Creator as one again, as it was in the beginning. The radiance has been shown throughout time but may be best known by the depictions of that soul known as the Christ in religious art. A surrounding of energy, in color, in intensity, with variations of content and in reality, variations in purpose as well.

There are many examples of people seeing aura even if they are not directly aware of it. We use color references often to describe attributes of the aura such as "in the pink" for vitality, and at the same time, pink is the color of youth. Green, when clear and pleasant as a color is that color for health and for wealth. Higher spiritual contact is often depicted as purple and that same color is the color of royalty, given attributes of that connection. Most people at most times are of a clear, white aura or a lovely blue, and the optimistic among us are gold. There are many colors and not all are pleasant.

Drug use and illness or such concerns as dehydration will cause a radiance of dark color, such as black, or dark brown for serious injury which might be the color of someone after such trauma as surgery. Intensity of color is also a factor in reading aura, sometimes the colors roll from one color to another and it is truly lovely to see this kind of event, while radiance will be greater or lesser according to the strength of the person as depicted by their physical energy at that moment. A well rested person has a bright aura, a person fatigued dims in the radiance, literally, and if stressed a dirty appearance occurs.

From my own experience, I know that there are several types of auras. One of the most dramatic was after I was touched by the Hand of God.

I have been touched twice, once at the moment just before traveling down the tunnel to the other side having just seen my past lives, and the second time while standing in my kitchen.

It was just an evening like any other in Tennessee and the unexpected touch gave me a view of auras unlike any I had seen previously.

Standing in my kitchen in the evening, my thoughts distracted only by the evening news as I prepared to cook dinner, there was a sharp rap or whack on my right shoulder. Imagine if you cupped your fingers together and you wanted someone to give you their attention. To accomplish this, you might just touch or lightly hit a person to get that person to look at you. That was much like what occurred to me except that the touch was firm and on target. My shoulder was touched just at the place where the neck line comes to meet the muscles of the shoulder. Put your own hand on your shoulder and you'll almost immediately know exactly where the touch of God occurred.

His Hand came down and as it did I immediately felt a pressure and I felt myself go down to my knees. A most wonderful feeling enveloped me that gave me warmth, hope, cleansing, and exhilaration all at once. As I reached out to steady myself by grasping the kitchen counter I saw my hands that then appeared strange and extended. The flesh of the fingers had not changed but the aura that emanated went several inches out, almost as if light formed knives that extended from those fingers. This was special, this was not a single color of aura, but a predominate dark blue, a cobalt blue of clear distinct color, with white stripes and even with dots of other colors imbedded in the light. It was truly an incredible sight. The feeling that accompanied the Touch of God is beyond description—a cleansing, a healing, a feeling of incredible euphoria but one of thanks and of praise.

This touch gave me something, as all of my contacts with God have given me something, but I am without the words or understanding to express what that gift might be. I am but a pinpoint of all that there is—the bulk is there, but it is as if I were attempting to put a tremendous amount of anything into a container and I am able to grasp only the smallest amount—that left over is all about me, but still just out of reach. This was the most incredible of auras ever observed—at least to this point—but there are more.

Circumstance seems to dictate what I am going to see when it comes to auras. I recall a person who wanted to speak to me about a problem he was having with a neighbor and he was livid about the circumstance. It ate at him, he chews on the words of every discussion, there was no escaping the pain and discomfort that effort to settle a disagreement with this neighbor brought to this person, a man in his mid-forties with a wife and family. This man wanted so much to be rid of the anger that pervaded his every day, his every move.

As we spoke, I saw clearly an aura that was first, solid. There was nothing I could see beyond this aura as it seemed solid—it was not the rolling color, nor was it the bright glow, nor a sense of energy normally seen. No, this was perhaps nine inches to twelve inches of solid color around his head, and exhibited points. The shape of the aura went on beyond being something that simply emanated to something that bore a shape as well. In this case, five distinct points were present.

As I spoke with the person, and I am clearly not the ministerial type though I do my best when called on to help where I can, it became clear that there were "points" of contention that needed to be addressed to understand this man's anger. He described issues that were personal affronts—so strongly opposed to his rigid "Christian" thinking in this East Tennessee town that anger was the only way for him to deal with his feelings. I was rational in my approach, objective rather than subjective. Feelings carry so much baggage that to approach issues in that manner only foul the works—I prefer to look at the facts and acknowledge whether the outcome of those feelings are valid or if in fact, those feelings are the problem.

The approach was to list those five points which was easy once we both understood the reason for their existence. As we talked I made notes and I jotted down the first issue the man had with the neighbor, then continued onto the second, and finished finally with the fifth. Laid out in that manner, we discussed the issues and saw how they intertwined and why failing to look at them objectively led to the accumulated angst and awkward dealings. The man seemed relaxed and focused when we parted, and since I did not know him personally I can't say if the issues were resolved, but I can say that progress had been made. The surprise in this observation of the aura was that the aura itself provided an approach to the resolutions of the problems.

In 1989 while in Tennessee, I had the good fortune to come into contact with a Professor from East Tennessee State University in Johnson City. It was a casual introduction that began with a group of friends who were involved in a Spiritual Study Group—in as much as souls do tend to incarnate in a group, I was certainly not surprised by our mutual interest in understanding our relationship to God.

We met weekly, and it seems that persons of unusual talent were always coming to discuss their take on topics that surprised me. For most part, the persons were well qualified such as a man just slightly younger than I who had the talent of meditating and dreaming in numerical symbols. Whereas I will dream and the events seem more literal, and related to past, present, and future, his revelations occurred at any time, and were not pictures (or visions) as most of us enjoy, but information was conveyed to him with circles, squares, vectors, Greek letters, and the like, all currently used in the study of mathematics. He shared some of his understanding with us, and while some was just beyond my and some others in the group understanding, there were other persons who at least claimed to get the gist of the information. It seemed more precise, we were told, in knowing details of what the future would hold.

It was from this group of prior-incarnation friends, back again for this karmic round that the introduction to the professor came. Ever since my experience with seeing my past lives, I've wanted to know about each one. Every face explored was a story, and every lifetime completed a building block to understanding my direction in this lifetime. The professor was very skilled in the art of hypnosis. We did not discuss it as there seemed so much to talk about, but I had learned that she would put her entire class into a hypnotic state (with their permission, of course) as a study aid. Quite the skilled practitioner.

This was a great opportunity and I was delighted to have the opportunity to have arranged a session. The session would be conducted at her home on a Saturday, and the meeting was eagerly awaited.

Arriving at the home set back from the road after driving from Kingsport to Johnson City gave me the impression of utter peace. A nice home, older like many of the homes in the area, but well kept and reflecting more of the southern style of a hundred years ago than this date or decade even.

There were other persons there which surprised me for some reason, I was not expecting other people to be present but that would not deter me from this session and I followed instructions as we began.

An arbitrary selection of a life "two hundred years ago" was what was made and this being 1989, the goal for life review was 1789. A nice round number, I agreed, and we all went on with the regression.

Laying slightly back while sitting on a sofa, I carefully followed the instructions of the professor and soon found myself almost overcome by the peace and rhythm that was being created by her voice. No big dramatic move, nothing at all like the event where I saw all of my past lives or traveled down the tunnel to the other side. No, this was easy and quiet and I felt secure and warm as I sat there. Soon, my head drooped and my eyelids sagged and I found myself looking at a scene, I'm assuming, somewhere in 1789. I knew where it was and I saw another person.

The location was on the East Coast of England and I owned a large amount of land and was a gentleman farmer—I stood there tall and slim and wore a tailored suit. The suit appeared light blue and I spoke with a woman who I knew was my wife. We seemed happy but the relationship was a bit more stilted, a bit more formal—and she was shorter and wore ruffled clothing consistent with the times from what I have seen in historical movies. There was not a special attention to time or event in that the professor and I had simply selected the year, and I was not drawn to this time and place for any reason other than to experience the effect of hypnosis. After a period where I seemed to examine details of that time and place, I felt myself being drawn back to the present time as the professor ended the hypnosis session. Noting the detail of the regression and the fact that the regression had even been successful, I chalked the day up as a success.

The regression became relevant again in 1990 and I had moved from East Tennessee to Miami. Work was not as rewarding as I had hoped in East Tennessee, and having lived in Sarasota a few years earlier, I was anxious to get back to the warm sun and tropical breezes.

The warm sun burns if you are not careful, and a prolonged stay in the tropical breezes will leave you poorly conditioned for the constant heat of the day and night—but I liked Florida and hoping for better work opportunities, I headed for Miami which is a year-round city where I had an aunt to who would welcome me for a brief stay while I established myself.

This was the south side of South Florida, near an area called Perrine and just south of Palmetto High School, and I learned of an adult education center in the high school. Hoping to meet some people and perhaps drawn to one particular course offered there, I chose to look into the classes. The class that interested me was ESP and Parapsychology. This was not graded class but few persons who signed up for the class failed to attend regularly, and it was relaxed and an opportunity for a lot of people to share their personal experiences related to experiences involving extrasensory perception. The parapsychology aspect was instructed by a gentleman and covered a number of subjects including pyramids, reincarnation, and other related subjects.

We met weekly and it was a wonderful way to connect with other people in that area of South Miami. One of the attendees was Joanne Yoham, a flight attendant.

Joanne was a very pleasant person, her astrological sign was Scorpio and she was about my age. It was through the class that we were introduced—this time. Joanne and I enjoyed the class and we lapped up the lectures in that room. Because of her job, Joanne missed a few classes, though I did my best to attend them all. It was one day when we were on a break that I had the time to actually talk to her and it was a pleasant talk. At the time I knew that I could see auras as I had learned in to do so in the spiritual study group I enjoyed in East Tennessee—one of the simple tasks I can teach others to do that has a definite psychic bent to it. With Joanne though, a different type of aura from the others I had experienced. We knew love—a deep and abiding love from the lifetime in 1789 when life was more simple, morals more definite, and a wandering eye for us a non-issue, I loved her and in God's wisdom I was to see that again.

Joanne's aura was almost as that generally portrayed with the Virgin Mary—solid and round, and in her case the color pink indicating love— and there was a real thrill seeing it.

The color pink conveys either a love, a love connection, or in the case of children, youth. Seeing aura is almost like feeling mood and sentiment often, a delightful combination of information, feelings, and often future. And perhaps the best part, a simple method to learn to see auras requires only perhaps six to eight people.

That would be three or four to serve as the observed, and the other three or four to serve as the observers. The roles are then reversed so that the observed become the observers, and the observers become the observed. The distinctive part of Joanne's aura in this experience was that it had definite edge, and was opaque. Aura generally is a rolling color of one or another, and is transparent or semi-transparent.

As in the case of anger, and this of love, the really strong emotions seem to be solid as opposed to the soft surrounding of color.

There too is that experience of aura that conveys problems and one experience of that was following a surgery of my cousin, a female, in East Tennessee. That experience showed me a dark brown aura, streaked with white and light color beams, but also conveyed a taste in my mouth which could only be described as the foul taste of the odor of death. Extreme trauma to the body can produce a sense so strong that taste can also result.

One last but very important example of aura that I must share. During a period of extreme meditation lasting several months that I meditated from as many as two to four times per day usually consisting of a solid one to two hours of meditation, I achieved a very high energy level. The result of that meditation was an energy force that was at least golden in color, radiating outwards in a wavy stream that ended in a white light radiance that seemed to have a definite edge to it.

That radiance was translucent and that meant that objects beyond the energy was visible. This energy produced by intense meditation was a different kind of energy—more akin to the power of God than to the energy generated by an individual's soul.

Be cautioned though—there are those individuals who can see this, and they are common, who will simply brush against you to steal the energy you have acquired. Stay clear of those persons, and be cautious of those who seek you out to take your energy. Those persons seek not only your energy, but the very power you possess to bring about positive change in your own life. I have had to tell more than one person I come in contact with on a daily basis not to touch me, and have had energy stolen by persons who will come up behind you without warning to intentionally take your energy.

Sitting quietly one day in a twelve-step meeting, a sudden burst of energy seemed to fall on me from above. The radiance surrounded me and enveloped my arms, hands, fingers and all that I could see of myself. Even my sight seemed to light up with the energy burst. No one else could see it, or so I thought, but I quickly learned how wrong I was. A person sitting just a few chairs behind me revealed himself as he almost immediately moved from his seat, intentionally brushing against me with the purpose of stealing my gift of energy.

Feeling the rapid drain of energy, I quickly turned to my right to see this person walking quickly to the kitchen area of the room, my energy radiating from him in a distinct pattern. Not an aura, but literally waves of energy emanating from his body. Stolen, but not lost I realized, as I mentally asked my guides, my guardian angels to rectify this wrong.

I soon saw this person slumping in his seat as the meeting progressed, the bright of the energy now revealing a downtrodden dark look on this person. I didn't take joy in his loss but realized that not only had the stolen energy been removed from him, but a sizeable amount of what energy he had already possessed had gone too. And as the days passed, this reported how poorly he felt. I did not believe that sympathy was in order for this person, after all, the loss of his energy was self inflicted. Perhaps there was a lesson to be learned, I only hope this person learned it well.

Chapter Twenty

There are those too, who have advanced themselves so spiritually that they are in contact with their guides easily, and can see the future for great distances of time, though may still choose to disregard the principles set forth by God.

They pursue for their own material gain at the expense of others. One, who I will refer to only as Tim, was once a personal assistant for a very well known and wealthy performer, from a family of performers, forefront in the music industry.

This person found me and I thought it was a blessing as the time of my life was difficult. Bobo had directed me to California but became even more of a problem once we arrived here. While Bobo was going in and out of the justice system—not court, but being sent to rehabilitation centers to deal with his persistent drug use this person, Tim, found me first on the internet, then appeared quite unexpectedly to me in a thrift shop near my home.

I recognized the person almost immediately, and our short conversation established a means to further contact each other. It was easy to recognize him, with long flowing locks of hair, and a large body but a soft demeanor. For a man this large, it was funny to hear him giggle, but that is the personality that accompanied the body this time around.

He told me that in his last lifetime he was a female prostitute, an attitude adjustment had been made in this lifetime and he was far more prim and proper, having engaged the lessons learned between lifetimes regarding his moral compass—at least those relating to sex. It was not the case for integrity apparently.

Being new to the area, this was Palmdale, California, and having Bobo going in and out of the system due to drug use, I was looking for a friend that was not a burden and Tim had established a group that invited gay men for social contact—nothing more than that fortunately, and there seemed an opportunity for me to break out of the isolation and the total focus that Bobo's drug use and problems had me focused on.

I was likely an easy mark and I even assumed, though erroneously, that this person with the highly developed psychic abilities had been sent to assist me. I should have been more aware of the answer when I asked Tim if that was the case, and he had said no. Having had so much direct interaction with Metatron in the short few months before meeting Tim, I was hoping and perhaps even expecting more assistance to come to deal with the difficulties I bore for Bobo.

I became friends with Tim and met others in this gay men's social group in the area, even attending a Gay Pride event in downtown Palmdale.

Small by comparison to other events in San Diego and certainly San Francisco for Gay Pride, no unexpected as the population in the Palmdale and Lancaster area is much smaller too, and there is no real gay life save a small bar in Lancaster.

There were even events at Tim's home—particularly a Halloween party that was an annual event, and Tim took great effort to decorate his home in the ghoul and goblin motif, even introducing me to his mother who lived with him and who too had a great deal of psychic development and ability.

All seemed well but appearances can be deceiving. We built a friendship I thought, but Tim's purpose was never far from center of the relationship. In early 2011, my guides had come to me and made a promise, an announcement that I was to be the beneficiary of their kindness and details were explained that were to transpire in the near future, along with a move to Palm Springs.

Even then, I was told that Tim would attempt to steal for his own purpose the gifts that God was sending to me, and I was a bit surprised to learn that. At the same time, my guides continued with that information and told me that "they would take care of it from that side" and I rested comfortably with that information.

The nature of the gifts must remain shrouded to allow the outcome to materialize still, my guides also told me of other upcoming events to occur in Palm Springs.

One event was a job for me. I'm getting used to doing God's work and am more apt to throw caution to the wind as I do my task. For one reason alone I will go forward if no other reason exists: in all that is to be done, the work is for God and therefore a benefit to my personal spiritual advancement, the core purpose of my existence on earth.

Another reason too is that failure is never failure. Should I lose my life as I do the work for God then what have I lost? Nothing for sure, for my soul is eternal and my return to God immediate. What is the worst that could happen to me other than my life ends, I review and prepare for the next phase of my development, then reincarnate for the next new life or take on the task that may be for my betterment and eventual return to God?

The preparation given me by my guides was so precise that even though I could not grasp the name of an individual I was to help, I could grasp the phone number of the person I was to help. Literally, my guides gave me a phone number that would have absolutely confirmed that the right person was there to receive the message that I was to deliver. I woke from the state that exists between sleep and wake to converse with my guides that evening with a firm knowledge of that person's telephone number and a message of caution to be delivered. I had been given area code, exchange, and number—I could have picked up my phone and dialed the number to speak to the person I was going to meet in the future had that been my task, but the time was not yet.

The caution was clear—avoid drug use or lose all that you have. Seemingly this was a simple message but for this person, it might be a critical crossroad in his life. A description of a course of events was delivered and this course of events included use of existing drugs, personal habits and sexual mores, and the warning of new drugs to be introduced which would be found in his body causing a loss of job.

With this loss of job, home and health would both plummet and a spiral would ensue from which there would be no escape this lifetime. That was the warning, and it was not to be taken lightly.

It was in this same time period that my guides spoke of my spouse. The first introduction to my spouse was when I was 15 years of age and my guides gave me the image of my spouse, and the knowledge that it would be many years before I was to meet and be with this person who I loved already—from lifetimes past, who would be my rock, the delight of my soul, even if it were me to do the carrying. A burden of joy if a burden at all, a moment of contact that lasts an eternity, a dream made manifest—and all of this two years after my spouse's birth, to spare me being made aware of the fact that I was to be gay this lifetime, and unprepared to know of my sexuality while younger than my 15 years.

As the image filled my head I walked alone towards home, a quiet dirt road from a river-side day camp and weekend swim club, towards the street that led me to my house. The insects buzzing in the farmer's field, the warm sun of a summer day as the sun started its downward drift toward night. It was then that God let me know I was not to be alone nor unloved. I let the image and the knowledge sink in and it gave me comfort. There were many times when the tears flowed—I was always alone but knowing that God was there to catch the feelings gushing from me helped to dispel the loneliness.

Sometime in the 1980's I stole a glimpse of my spouse on television, he is—or as he now prefers—was a public figure, an accomplished athlete and I learned what he was doing with his life and I wondered if somehow our paths could cross sooner if I prayed, and pray I did. I did not know his name and lacking the resource of the internet as we have today, finding information was far more difficult and I had little to nothing to begin my search. I kept the image from the television in mind, but soon gave up on knowing more—I had been given a mere morsel as a reminder of my spouse but that was all I was to have for the time. My heart longed to know him but my hands had nothing to grasp.

As time went on, the issues of the day and the appearance of others in my life occupied my thoughts and effectively buried my concerns about my spouse. With others, it was not the love that I had hoped for—each person is so much more the person when love is part of the experience—but we deal with what we have to deal with. Friends, some good friends, others bordering on a simple acquaintance but perhaps with the hope for a fuller, more meaningful relationship intruded on my day and knowing that realization of the future with my spouse was so very far off, I allowed myself to move on.

It was part of the future detail given me in March 2011 while in Palmdale that revived the hope and reminded me of the knowledge of my spouse, bringing me to a longing unlike any other I have ever experienced. Love is very, very valuable, a commodity so needed and so wonderful that mere life is unlived without it. The touch, the memory, the scent of love can so overwhelm us that living can become unbearable without it. Time expecting the love of your spouse can be so distant that it becomes a great abyss—a chasm so wide that the last bit of courage is ripped from your heart waiting for the coming of the person. Then one day, perhaps without warning, your spouse enters the room and you know almost miraculously that your spouse has arrived.

The date was January 4th, 2012, and the time was 12:10 PM. As I sat at a table facing perpendicular to the room entrance that opened to the sidewalk on the back of the building, the door must have swung open unceremoniously as it neither was heard in this room full of people nor did I pay attention to just another arrival of a person entering the room. This though, was no ordinary entrance and it was an action that only God could have arranged, only God could have prepared, and only I could have felt the power that entered with that person. After all these years and with all the tears, my spouse had come from heaven and we shared the same room in the same lifetime.

As my spouse entered—note that I had not previously seen him in the flesh—I was engulfed by a new sensation and it was the Love of the Power of God and it unmistakably let me know that this was the person, this was the love of my life who had entered the earth plane after I did, and who God in his Wisdom gave me thought and wisdom that day in 1963 as I walked along the dirt road. Here now was that person, the one I would marry, the one I would love, who would love me for me, and for whom I would exclude all others to share in the joy of two souls breathing as one.

That was the power and the feeling and the sensation. I looked up almost in disbelieve and most certainly in confusion as the feeling pouring over me was unknown to me but it was compelling. My mind raced as I strained to see the person. This was a room full of people—a room where seating was available to anyone but the set up does not change.

A large table in the center dominates the room and the table is ringed by three seats on each end, and seven seats on either side and all the seats were filled. We are a popular room, friendships are made here and this is where God brought my spouse that day. The room has another five seats at one end that flank the door leading another way out and each side of the room has seventeen seats. More seats are in an open area between the kitchenette/coffee area and eight to twenty seats can be occupied in this area.

Today, two seats were open along the west wall and my spouse took one and immediately a person who is self-important and arrogant seats himself so to block my sight and perhaps to serve his own purposes. This intrusive person is psychic too, and a message from God that I delivered to him recently said of this person "you were given great gifts to help others and you chose to help yourself. As a result, you are to incur five additional incarnations over a span of two thousand years to resolve this karma."

God, it would seem, doesn't miss the fine points of spiritual advancement, and keeps tabs on all of us. The hard part was that the message given me to deliver had to be held for almost three months before the time of delivery. I observed the same clothing, weather, time, and surroundings as in the vision when the message came, and delivered the message right on cue and without hesitation or falter. That person was heavily impacted, but from my own observations I would question whether changes were made. God will decide, but I still see the same self-importance and arrogance in this person remaining. However, I am content that my job has been done and I can move on. This person will carry his own weight—the job is no longer mine to bear.

Whatever this self-important and arrogant person had done to deserve the delay in spiritual advancement no doubt earned the punishment. Just being in the position to know the actions of God from time to time gives me a perspective I would never had expected on earth, but I have a job to do for God and the tools and experiences I collect along the way are indeed surprising to me.

As my spouse sat down, I strained to see who was there, the energy enveloping him and me both confusing and empowering—I knew we were there to be together. The self-important and arrogant person sat down next to him, moving from a perch he had taken in the kitchenette and blocking my vision of my spouse. What arrogance!

As my spouse leaned forward unknowing of me in the room, the self-important and arrogant person leaned forward, as my spouse leaned back, the self-important and arrogant person leaned back. This process went on and on as the meeting flowed and the attendees unknowing of the drama playing out between three chairs in the room. The meeting finally ended and I briskly walked to meet the person who is my spouse, and again the self-important and arrogant person tries to interfere but the name of my spouse is acquired and even a reference to a YouTube video is suggested.

The great public image of my spouse is preserved in a format unknown at his and my birth and in the lifetimes before us. And I, missing him for so many years cry while watching the elegant and gracious moves executed by him as if moved by the Hand of God.

I am overwhelmed, and I am tongue tied and my heart is filled with joy but my spouse can't linger today, and after making more short social contacts he walks briskly to his car. I think of him and I can't wait for the next time that we will meet. I silently scow at the self-important and arrogant person and do my best to ignore this interloper. This same person had already annoyed me trying to touch me to steal the energy that God had so graciously given me, a crime accomplished by a mere touch of the hand or even the brush of a hair, a single hair even. While I often bob and weave to escape his subtle and not so subtle attempts to touch me, I have had to leap when a brash attempt to touch me has been his goal.

Finally, I did have to directly ask the self-important and arrogant person not to attempt to touch me and I did that when I delivered God's message. Still, as you might expect his attempts do continue. Perhaps it is senility and a failure of memory, but I suspect the arrogance simply prevails in his continued efforts. The energy vampires exist, and this person is far from the only one I know. Each and every of these scoundrels will make every effort to take that which has been given to you and you must be careful to avoid them.

Knowing of the wisdom of God, I can only pray that the rule of karma will apply here too. Are those so arrogant so unknowing of God's generosity that they will not seek to gain the energy that God so willingly provides by seeking to remove that energy that others have earned? Take all of what others have earned and learn that you've lost all that you have gained.

For the selfish and uncaring, be forewarned. God's law is perfect— either learn to bend to God's law or learn to lose by God's law, but you will not escape God's law. Know too that death does not release you from God's Law—on the contrary, you are brought full front to understanding and remembering God's Law, and you will prepare to reincarnate to again have the opportunity to apply God's Law as God intended.

On a practical note, bear in your heart and mind this protection: God's Light Surround Me. This is a simple but effective way to resolve the attempts and affronts of these psychic demons. And just thinking of God in a literal sense does draw you closer—though some people have longer path to be closer to God than others.

The ensuing weeks brought a hindering effect as my guides cautioned me "to be mellow with (spouse)" and not wanting to break the possibility of knowing my spouse in this lifetime, I found myself to be very, very tongue tied whenever I was even in sight of him, much less standing in front of him or trying to converse with him. Every evening my prayers were to ask God to make it all easier to know, to care, to hold him in my arms. I knew that it might take time but I also knew that it would happen. For if nothing else were to sustain me in knowing my spouse, knowledge of God does provide faith, whereas faith does not provide knowledge of God. Meditate, I beg of you, meditate! Let the truth be your guide but be cautioned that truth is the strangest of experiences possible. As you advance in your spiritual knowledge and with the wisdom of God as I have learned, there will be many souls incarnate who think you simply daft. "You need not believe me but I will tell you only the truth", has been my mantra and it does provide at least the opening to understanding to your listener though it is likely not immediate nor even soon, but as they learn the change to understanding is easier, and safer than being forced into reconsideration of tenets. Do read slowly, it will be a rocky road ahead.

For most part the seldom encounters with my spouse were fine—me usually floundering for a sensible word to say, something witty would have been wonderful but I didn't know his humor and I had no way to know his humor. I felt intimidated too thinking his social life abundant and busy and wondering how I was to fit in, me largely a wallflower unless I were leading the parade (or throwing the party) and this location, this current setting, not allowing me either funds nor property to carry through on such things. No doubt on the mark, one of my sent spiritual advisers told me once that I had reached the very bottom of my group when it came to my wealth.

That means that with careful budgeting, I would have a roof over my head and I would eat, but even gas was to be used sparingly especially since the price of gas had soared across the country and my pocketbook had a bottom that I could easily see. I wondered how many more things could have been a problem but relied on the knowledge that God provides. Was I wrong to say to God "if you provide, why so sparingly?" That's fine though. I'm being tested I'm sure, and boy, do I ever hope I'm scoring well. I do rely on God for all things. It must be that change in attitude that will help me at least in the afterlife even if the material world lacks just a bit of the material goods that would add comfort and convenience to the incarnation.

My last incarnation was sparse in material goods too—a Cambridge Professor, and a speaking tour or two, and reliance on sponsors for most of my skill and craft that provided little in the way of income. Not your blue ribbon investments, it seems.

My spouse came into and out of my life and I often wondered what his daily life was. I assumed a busy social schedule, important business dealings and a whirlwind of contacts though I never saw him out and about. No wonder there, my travels are pretty much limited to walking the dog and the infrequent trips once to twice a month for groceries.

There is a very nice grocery store within a a short walk of my home, but I rely on Tuesday's circulars to plan my purchases. Any way you slice it today, I must be frugal. Always enough to survive but not enough to waste, but my gratitude to God is for that which he gives, not anger for that not given. There has been so much to keep me hoping and anticipating my spouse—the energy I feel when near, the dreams that disclose and explain, a very strange event that brought me knowledge of his love that arrived, of all places, over the internet.

I am not much of the social media—just beyond the age of where I would have been involved in it as it started and grew, and too old to really care about all the angst of the younger set. I did find my spouse's Facebook page though—Facebook is just wonderful to find old friends as there is no repository save the Social Security Administration of the United States Government to find someone, and clearly the Social Security Administration does not give access to its records. That is what it is and that is how it goes. But I found my spouse on Facebook and I am thinking that I dare not even let him know that I checked. I'm not a stalker, but I am resourceful person and I have to carefully tread that line. If I'm looking for one person and a simple search engine request provides a number of pictures, details, even videos posted, is that stalking? I think not. On the other hand, if I am trying to stand outside the persons door or meet his friends or arrange "accidental" meetings, then yes, I am intruding on that person's life and that is stalking. How do I meet my spouse? I go to my meetings and just hope he shows up. I even know a couple places where he regularly attends other meetings and he has, within my group, publically made that statement and I chose not to intrude there where I know he will be. As I said, it's a fine line between inquisitive and intrusive, and I put my head to sleep each night with many questions unanswered and that is fine with me though certainly not desirable. The right outcome will come in time, and that is getting ever closer. Besides, how can I come to live with myself if my actions are dishonest and my desire is an honest relationship? The only way is to keep my actions always honest and then there is no reason for self-doubt.

As the few months passed, I found myself becoming the tormented of my own torment. First, I had taken a course of action to bring myself to a state achieved by frequent meditation and often denying myself the opportunity to go to these meetings. What incredible experiences I had—the sheer energy of God coursing through my body. My chakras, especially my head chakra, nearly aflame each day and my spiritual advisor telling me that the feeling of my energy could be felt miles away. That tells me that I had elevated myself above the level of most persons on the earth plane and it was during that time that so many people seemed to seek me out apparently as a result of that energy whether they knew or did not know why. My spouse drove a distance away from my home at one point and our connection was so strong that I turned to see him go by though he probably didn't know I was there but I unmistakably knew he was there.

Then there were two other events when his mere entry into the room of the twelve step program again resulted in the incredible energy and feeling that first exhibited itself on the Fourth of January, 2012.

Just a day following the last experience of energy that occurred on the 30th of July 2012, I got a call from my spouse. Oddly on the 30th I was occupied in a way that prevented me from approaching my spouse and he seemed distracted and quickly left the room following the meeting. Though we still have no relationship at this time beyond a casual acquaintance, I called. It was the first time ever I had called and it was short—I was interrupting him as he entered someplace for lunch with a friend, he said. Perhaps my timing was just wrong.

The following day though I got a shocking call in return and my spouse called to see if I was available to meet him for a late breakfast. My reply and action was fast and of course, I accepted the meeting. For the first time ever, we spoke at length and decided to carry on the day together, me going along on his rounds as proprietor of a specialized property management company, then breaking as he took the reins of a class he conducts locally. The day included the attempt to make a large purchase and he appreciated my assistance and support as the steps required for the purchase were examined and evaluated. Though we—rather he—chose not to go forward at that time, we did discover that we worked well together. My lifting the spirit of the day and he pondering the impact of the decisions required. He told me that he felt very compelled that day to call me—I was hoping that his guides were doing the same push that mine were. After all, we had the same goal, though I have to say, having the foresight to the future make me immediately amiable to the arrangement, but I'll have to earn my spouse's love and respect before we fully connect.

My guides have already discussed several potential outcomes with me for my romantic association, and I'm comfortable with them all though impatient for the start of my life with him. I see that as happiness, a final and solid time for the embrace of hope, happiness, and shared dreams. I am willing to wait if I must. Do I have any other choice, after all?

Still, the relationship is awkward and confusing—an invitation one day and a demand to not overstep boundaries the next, though no real introduction of change anywhere in between. That is OK though—perseverance is personal trait of mine and it has served me well. Not doggedly persevering, but kindness and patience in what I do. My spiritual advisor has said with incredible insight that nothing comes easy for me, and I know that but never formed the words in my own mind until I heard them. So true, so confoundingly true. If I knew why that is the case, if I could understand why such challenges always beset me demanding such extra effort, such devotion to purpose, perhaps acceptance would be easier for me but I must trudge, push, plan, and motivate myself for what little achievement I am able eke out. If not for the solid accomplishment held, I surely would be saddened, perhaps broken by the effort needed to add but one success to my belt. Almost as if it takes every step again to climb the mountain, one, two, three times and even then, should success be mine?

Chapter Twenty One

I want to look now at the last time I climbed the mountain—that mountain being Mount Everest and me being known as George Herbert Leigh Mallory, the Cambridge Professor and Lecturer, and the Mountaineer. This time, we move from a general review to the specific morning of June 8, 1924. I had a birthday coming up on June 24, 1924 and I would have turned 38 years of age and it would have been, should have been a celebration of incredible accomplishment.

Thirty seven years was all that I would make of that lifetime, abruptly losing my life that bright morning in the clear, thin air at the top of the world.

Sandy Irvine was to accompany me and he was selected because he had great physical strength, and at least agreed to be agreeable to instruction as we went up the mountain. There were only two of us, Sandy holding the camera that was to record the conquest of the highest point on earth as I, George Herbert Leigh Mallory, generally being acknowledged as the most competent and fiercely determined Mountaineer on the planet, to topple the last horizon. If others did not think of me that way or know of my quest, let no one even suggest that I did not think of myself that way. I was incredibly determined and I was incredibly competitive but not against my companions, but against the forces of nature—the real foe in the real world.

Mankind by God's virtue may band together to achieve so much and it is God's will that we do so, but we are left with the earth to remain a great challenge to our success, and we to challenge the common enemy beneath our feet.

Our day's journey started out early and we had prepared the night before to leave in the dark. Save the light of the stars, there was little else to guide us, but our packs were ready and we had forged a purpose that was unadorned and direct, an accomplishment waiting that would be a crowning achievement for man and men. Having no real reason to stir the others on our expedition, we chose not to disturb them and quietly left our camp without fanfare or goodbyes. Those that woke merely acknowledged our departure, discussion of the event having hours past settled into plan and expectation. It was an unceremonious start to what was to be a grand accomplishment.

Sandy and I climbed well that dark dawning morning, stopping only for the requisite moments needed to collect our thoughts, and let our bodies catch up with our enthusiasm—this was a job to be done and we applied all of the steps for our safety and success as we walked, footfall after footfall, grasp after grasp. This was to be the final leg, and I played my script in my head. It was to be documented by photograph, it was to be an act of success of the team but I was fortunate to be the headstone, my name inscribed in the history books for that conquest of the greatest frontier, and an act of love to honor my ever patient, ever loving wife, Ruth. The highest point on earth dominated by the men who so form the land and seem to even make bow the tide if it were their will.

Man would be indomitable as he had so often before. We conquered our land, then we conquered our sea, now we challenge even the fortress of the mountains that had defied us.

As Sandy and I trudged forward and upward the looming peak became more defined, the edges cutting the sky in a way that became personal. We moved comfortably and in rhythm breathing the thin air and it chilled our lungs and our toes ached from not only the frigid ground, but from the crunch that turned our toes upward each time our foot sought a place to rest on the giant of the earth. The human foot was not designed to be used the way we used it—contorted by the land beneath it, and twisted by the often sideways push of gravity and the downward sliding of our upward moves. Nature placed these obstacles before us and there was no way to escape the barriers—we had only the option to conquer. If that were cold, we persisted. If that were pain, we endured. Uncomfortable was merely the state of existence but not a reason to delay, to falter.

Careful placement gave us a connection to the wildlife of the world like the mountain goat who at least had the sanity to know limits while we sought only to exceed those limits if we even cared to acknowledge them. No, we were mountaineers and only the conquest of the mountain would signal our success.

The dawn broke clearly and the rays of the sun shown in a way that gave glory its name. As if above us and below us light raced to meet the uprushing land and the edge of the universe that seemed to set only a short distance from us. Far below and beyond us other peaks sat in judgment waiting for our efforts to continue, but the sun greeted us with warmth and finally, with awareness of our moves.

We stood in the radiance of the new day, it was the eighth of June and the year was 1924. Today, the conquest of Mount Everest would be added to man's name, a fitting piece of history for his adornment. The frontier of the my life succeeded and conquered. I would have much to talk about to my colleagues and it would be honorable and interesting.

An achievement that would be mine until my death, as we all must die, and I looked forward to reaching that end with the love of my wife, and the glory brought by my loving children. A life lasting until my muscles drooped, my hair grayed, and my eyes saw only the memories of my life.

Below us lay the base camp from which we had left hours before in the darkness of the night to be here as the sun broke. Looking down gave us no direction nor did it give us concern. A cloud cover had moved in but it seemed to envelope only Everest—beyond was brilliant that morning, and we reveled as light touched each peak, each valley, and from our height, we were sure we saw rivers too but so much sparkled that you could not tell water from ice, and greens, grays, browns and more gave a pallet to the horizon that only God could have painted. We knew our expedition would be watching for us that morning but we also knew that they would have to wait to greet us on our return.

God saw us now and no one else had the eyes to see through the haze of the blanket of clouds below us. I wondered if the camp were enveloped too—it could easily have reached down that far. The cold of a cloud bank is almost beyond description: damp, dark, unbearable and depressing.

Success should be cheered, not endured and weather plays a part when it makes itself known—had it only chosen to be quiet today, I would have loved to wave to my friends below if only they might have seen me. The effort might be fruitless but it would be satisfying. Mother Nature was unforgiving, but God blessed us in his glorious morning.
We continued the climb and did so steadily and determined to reach the height before us. The sheer thought of the success would have taken our breath away had it not been for the thin air already depriving us. Our bodies were conditioned though, by years of effort and purpose, me getting on in my years even at 37, nearly 38, and wanting the conquest so much. My younger companion, only 22, was support for my efforts, and I felt a resource if youth were the factor in our efforts. His reward would be the history books, as would mine, and the crag against the sky our trophy.

An outcropping before the final push gave us a place to rest and the clear blue sky gave us mid-morning clarity. We rested for a period before starting that last bit of effort that would cap the expedition and finally summit the highest point on earth. Not one to shy away from a good photograph, I asked Sandy to take several photos as I made that final push for the summit. Each upward step is a determined move and must be carefully planned and calculated lest all our efforts be unrewarded through foolish neglect. Not me, I thought, not this place would deny us.

Our purpose had to be blessed by God for we had health and determination and we knew our true benefactor. Fearing only a waste of time, we rose and carefully started forward, loosely tethered to each other as the final effort was made. I arranged my clothing for that appearance of nonchalance though not a single button, strap, or pocket failed to have a purpose—and my promise to my wife ready. I gingerly set my cleats as each foot doggedly sought the placement to lift me to the top. One hand taking anything to grasp, the other holding the pick that I used to bring support for the weight of my body as I raised it ever higher. My eyes were focused before me and the soil seemed incredible—I wondered how so much of Mother Earth could have piled so high, to give me purpose in my effort, to show the world our success. In my pocket I bore the altimeter, a small instrument that let me know that my climb had passed the clouds—more a curiosity than anything, but an instrument that I could reference for our efforts and for the problems we encounter.

Breathing was making us slower but determination kept us moving forward. I fingered the piece and looked at it. It read over 8,000 meters and I slipped it back into my pocket. I would not make me successful, it could only tell me that I had been successful. My efforts must continue.

Slowly I climbed keeping keen focus on my upward steps. Soon I could feel the exhilaration of nearing my mark and I turned slowly around to Sandy, now several meters below me and he stood there with hands folded behind him. How odd, I thought, I could not call out for the lack of oxygen, and the distance too, would make my efforts a waste, but I wanted to see that camera poised to record the conquest of the summit. Did the photograph not seem appropriate at this point? Perhaps if I took even a greater effort to give a climbing pose and if I moved perhaps another meter, or even less, then the right appearance might give Sandy the signal to click the shutter on this historic moment.

I grasped what I could in my left hand carefully drew up my feet, planting again the cleats into the odd soil. Moving my body upward was a full effort: plant feet then push up carefully, maintaining a simple rhythm of push, grasp, set climbing pick and repeat. The climbing pick was my safeguard—setting it firmly into the soil was imperative and I looked for the most accommodating place with the firmest soil to do that. There had to be always someplace to accept the long intrusion of the pick, my weight bore on that small instrument, and my life depended on it too.

Moving up a bit I felt the warmth of the sun on me and I turned again, hoping finally that Sandy had picked up the camera to record this near end of our journey—the conquest of Mount Everest. Carefully turning I realized my pose would look great even if not the most prudent of actions to take. My feet well set, my left hand slightly below the equator, the point where my balance was precarious as my hand should be above the middle of body, and the higher the better. My right hand held the pick as if in mid-thrust, ready to set and secure. I managed a smile as I gingerly turned my head to look back, my eyes swinging to my left carefully following the slow turn of my head but sighting Sandy, he still stood there.

I didn't even see the camera and I didn't appreciate the humor if that was his intent. At this crucial point, I would have expected the closer adherence to our plan, not a rogue approach to his efforts. Had I not given him this place in history to claim and there were not second chances to be had.

My patience was wearing thin and I turned again as I had need to set my pick to keep my precarious balance on the side of the mountain. My personal discomfort was nothing to bear, but I needed to assure that each move was carefully and expertly executed. I held the pick in my right hand and used my strength to swing it into the side of the mountain with only the shortest of distances above me yet to scale. I felt the failure before even the sound reached my ears.

My arm thrust back and my balance wavered as the sound, a clink that could have been from the Bells of Saint Mary enveloped my ears. My hand had nothing to hold me, the tip of the pick had failed to lodge and the mountain had fought me. My arm wavered in mid air and my left hand, barely holding onto a crag defied me as my body moved back ever so slowly in my mind, but so quickly against the gravity that bore down on me.

I had failed to find a spot to set my pick and instead hit a frozen bit of earth—ice that rejected me as surely as a spurned love.

I sat in the cool morning air, my feet touching the challenge before me but my torso without the wings that I needed now. I was falling backward and had nothing to hold on to and below me was not the outcropping but a sliding of earth that would take me a thousand meters or more down without stop. I was falling. Surely it looked to Sandy Irving as if I were diving from the mountain, but as the adventurer I said to myself "I must turn. I'm not going to miss this even as I go to my death; I will not miss this adventure."

My feet still touched the mountain and I used that position to turn my body so that my fall was not buttocks first, but as if God had given me wings. I was to face my own demise and it was my will to do so but life would have been a better choice had it been an option. God's grace of that life did not see this as suicide, just an adjustment so I could add the experience to my life record. Suicide had been the fact in one lifetime— and God knew the truth now. I could not stop my death and I had not willed it either. God knows the heart and he knew mine.

I quickly left the thought of Sandy behind me as the wind whipped past my ears and my thought turned to a symbolic act—the picture of my loving wife Ruth in my breast pocket over my heart where I always carried it. The picture was to be the first item placed on the summit of Mount Everest as a symbol of my love for Ruth, and her devotion to me for all the absence and patience she endured caring for our home, our children, and no doubt the loneliness as she held her head high while her husband traveled the globe in search of glory and adventure. I reached into my pocket and felt the thin paper and pulled it out carefully so to not damage it. I was going to hold that image in my hand and if and when my body was found, it would be known that my thoughts were first, foremost, and lastly, for my darling Ruth.

What cruelty I thought as my arm extended to hold that paper before my eyes. The whipping wind took her from me as my grasp failed and the picture suddenly seemed to jump above me, lost into the air as I reached for it but failed in my effort. Today was not a good day, I recalled, I lost the mountain, I lost my life, and now I'm losing my Ruth. The sound of air rushing and the sound of the flapping paper echoed in my ears and I seemed confounded by it all as I rushed toward the ground. Clouds could be grasped easier than the picture—history would find it, I hoped.

Wait! I could show my accomplishment yet! Let me let all others know that I had reached the top. My altimeter was in another pocket and I reached for it. My fall was only a few short moments, I was sure, but seemed to be moving in slow motion or else my mind had learned to move much faster than I had ever experienced. It reached for the small instrument and I maneuvered it in my hand so it too did not fly away as my lovely Ruth had done. I can set this for the height we achieved,

I thought, by pressing the indicator into place for others to see. That, I reasoned, would let the world know we had gotten far. Close enough to almost touch God's heaven, and if providence saw fit, we could even have touched God.

I maneuvered my fingers in quick effort to set the marker on the altimeter with the wind still rushing. "This will tell them", I thought, "of our accomplishments!" The marker was thin, and it was frail, and there was only the slightest heft to the piece. It was only an instrument, it was not a tool, and in another profound disappointment, the marker flew to the universe. I didn't see it coming off but it was gone and I had no way to let the world know of my accomplishment. This too had been ripped from me, and I was saddened. It wasn't the loss of my life soon coming that disappointed me, it was failing to let the world know that we had almost reached the top.

I can't claim the success of the conquest of Mount Everest though that claim had been my purpose in this third expedition as had been my previous purpose for the first and second expeditions.

For me to be remembered I must be true to truth—it is sometimes hard to bear the burden of honesty but my responsibility is first to God, then to man, then to ego. God knows all, and won't let me stand before Him in sullied robe—no, to stand before Him at all I must go with truth and clear conscience. He knows all before I appear, does He not?

The claim of success is that of Sir Edmund Hillary for his 1953 conquest of the mountain and I challenge nothing of his efforts.

The wind tattered and pulled at my clothing as I continued to fall and there were three failures within moments that I bore. The ground seemed to rush toward me but yet was a great distance away. I wondered what the end would be like.

I didn't learn what the end would be like though as suddenly I floated in air—my still falling body below me and the buffeting of the wind gone. I didn't know what happened but I felt different, at peace and no longer concerned about what had been my fate.

The cold air no longer disturbed me but a warmth exuded and I could see more—I could see the future and I could see the past all at once and seemingly without limit and the present was my only point of reference.

Never before had I been this way I thought but there was scant time to ponder. I knew now the fate of Sandy Irvine and I wondered if somehow I would be able to help him.

Even as my body plummeted below me, I saw Sandy's demise. Sandy would live for 48 hours yet, but he would fall, really rather slide, into a crevasse on his attempt to get back to the base camp alone. My plan never included my own demise and I wondered now if my wisdom of bringing such an inexperienced climber with me in this most crucial effort was wise. From my vision of his future, that answer now seemed moot. His fate would be sealed and no one could be there to help him.

The essence of warmth emanated from two spots near me as I lingered there in air, still amazed by the transition and I glanced in that direction. Two spots of radiant light were near me and I instinctively knew them to be angels who had come for me. My soul was now separate from my body, and my thoughts, emotions, hopes and dreams all were tied to my existence but not to my earthly form. Without introduction, I asked "May I stay to help him?" referring to Sandy Irvine who I knew would soon leave this earth too and would like a helping hand to eternity. "No" they replied. It wasn't a sound but a feeling and with more clarity than any speech regardless of the eloquence, "no" was my direction and I thought again of Sandy's outcome.

Sandy would for about the next thirteen hours attempt to climb down— his own survival at stake and with the hopes to preserve his young life on earth. His future still more wanting than mine for I had achieved much. For thirteen hours he would gingerly place hand and foot to reach our companions below us. Those companions still camped but did not know of my demise nor did they see Sandy's careful effort to save his own life. The clouds still shielded them from the tragedy unfolding. There would come that moment in Sandy's life that he would hold against me, perhaps for a long, long time.

One mis-step would have Sandy slide down the side of the great Mount Everest but only for perhaps three meters but it would be without control and without chance for redemption—one leg lodged on one side of a rock that held him tight, and the other leg broken on the other side of the rock. Sandy's efforts stopped in such a short time, frustration of a life so short lived, frustration of an effort so quickly destroyed.

For the next twenty hours Sandy would struggle against the rock and the pain and the despair of an inability to free himself. Living exhaustion drains a man of hope, and Sandy's strength drained with the shackles of that rock. His spirit too would leave this earth that day, his body left behind to be found only in the dust of years to pass.

The effort to summit Mount Everest had ended for the two mountaineers seeking the adventure and the glory of the climb. Both souls had returned to our Creator, and each individually prepared for the next sojourn and period of advancement on Earth.

George Herbert Leigh Mallory returned to earth in 1948, the son of a truck driver and the child of a loving, oft associated mother in East Tennessee to resume the process of spiritual advancement once again.

Sandy Irvine was found too and we were associated in Florida in the early 2000's. I knew nothing of his soul's return but recognized him immediately when he walked into my office one day, and he walked in as my superior. Our association was often awkward, Sandy in his new form dubious of me, as I no doubt looked as if I had leapt from the side of Mount Everest as I turned to see my own fall. No, it was not suicide—I have had one incident of that and Heaven knows when that was. I left the company as a result of Sandy's new identity in 2006— exacting his revenge for having left him on the side of Mount Everest to die in 1924 even though I took no part nor did I wish the event to occur.

I have forgiven Sandy for his actions today, God has far too much for me to do today rather than to carry a grudge in this lifetime. I hope Sandy comes to that knowledge too.

This life is ongoing and there are many things yet for me to experience and to be in God's service. My spouse has yet to come to the understanding of our full relationship but I am comfortable of a positive outcome even though we presently are not even dating—and we may not see each other for a while. My guides have given me direction and that too is hope so I ask each day for God's Will and for the patience to carry that out. It will come.

Speaking of a past life or many past lives still causes many to be afraid but it should not. We are here to experience and to do so with God's Law held firmly to all that we do. We are born many times, and we will die just as many. This is schoolhouse earth and it has been prepared for us to learn and to grow. This is God's Kingdom and I am grateful that He has allowed me to serve Him in it.

This has been my story. Every word is true.

Index

M

Meditate 4, 153
meditation 4, 19, 26, 28, 48, 60, 61,
  62, 91, 93, 94, 95, 96, 98, 99,
  100, 101, 104, 105, 106, 107,
  108, 109, 110, 111, 143, 144,
  155
Metatron. *See* God
Miramar, Florida 10, 57, 113
Most High. *See* God
Mountaineer 157
Mount Everest vii, viii, 6, 40, 157,
  159, 161, 163, 164, 166

N

New Orleans 53
noble cause 116

O

orb 42
Orgy 56, 59
Osama Bin Laden 7

P

Pakistan 7
Palm Springs 124, 146, 147
Peter MacDonough 8
pick 26, 27, 54, 60, 69, 88, 132, 133,
  160, 161, 162
Plato 19, 20
Police Dispatcher 12
Presbyterian Church 6
prophesy 53, 79, 80, 81, 85, 123,
  125, 126, 128

R

Raymond Gale 80
reincarnation viii, 142
religion vii, viii, 4, 6, 24, 30, 73
Rusty 24, 25, 27, 28, 44
Ruth 158, 163

S

Saddam Hussein 7
Sandy 157, 158, 160, 161, 162, 163,
  165, 166
Sandy Irvine 157, 165, 166
Sarasota 17, 23, 29, 30, 31, 32, 33,
  35, 142
Sarasota, Florida 17, 23, 29
Secret Service 114, 115, 116, 117,
  118, 120, 121
self-hypnosis 4, 55
Senator Bob Graham 132, 135
Shelly 29, 30
Sheltie. *See* Rusty
Sherry 23
Shirley Carter 84, 131
silver cord 110, 111
snake 6, 55
sojourn on earth 2
soul vii, viii, 1, 3, 11, 14, 17, 27, 28,
  37, 38, 39, 40, 51, 60, 70, 71,
  73, 77, 78, 81, 83, 94, 99, 107,
  108, 109, 111, 137, 144, 147,
  148, 165, 166
soul mates 11
spiritual 2, 4, 10, 16, 19, 39, 52, 76,
  94, 108, 109, 137, 142, 147,
  150, 151, 153, 155, 156, 166
Spiritual Study Group 3, 140